Rocky Mountain National Park Trivia

John Daters

RIVERBEND
PUBLISHING

Dedication

To my mom—a woman who taught me to wade knee-deep in life's oddities and walk around a bit to see what happens. And to my unborn son, Evan Benjamin Daters, a little nugget of life, who I hope sees chuckle-worthy fun everywhere he cares to look.

Contents

Geography

Q. The headwaters of which three major rivers are found in the park?
a) The Colorado River, Cache la Poudre River and Big Thompson River
b) The Platte River, Cache la Poudre River and Gunnison River
c) The Colorado River, Cuyahoga River and Green River
A. c) The Colorado River, Cache la Poudre River and Big Thompson River.

Q. How many national forests border Rocky Mountain National Park?
a) One   b) Two   c) Three
A. b) Two: Arapaho National Forest and Roosevelt National Forest.

Q. What is the highest elevation in Rocky Mountain National Park?
a) 13,869 feet   b) 14,259 feet   c) 14,682 feet
A. b) The 14,259-foot-high Longs Peak provides the highest elevation within Rocky Mountain National Park. Often called a "14er," Longs Peak is one of Colorado's 54 mountains that stand 14,000 feet or higher.

Q. What is the lowest elevation in Rocky Mountain National Park?
a) 4,740 feet   b) 7,860 feet   c) 10,259 feet
A. b) The Cow Creek Trailhead, found in the northeast corner of

Rocky Mountain National Park, stands at 7,860 feet, the lowest point within the park.

Q. Did glaciation play a part in the area's geographic features?
A. Yes. Much of the park owes its geographic features to the epic impact of glacial movement.

Q. The features of Rocky Mountain National Park were partially created by the powerful movements of glaciers, which even today continue to shape the park. All glaciers fall into specific classifications; those still found in the park are exclusively categorized as cirque glaciers. What exactly is a cirque glacier?
A. Cirque glaciers, like those in the park, are relatively small and are found in bowl-shaped basins at the heads of mountain valleys. Usually, cirque glaciers are the leftover ice-forms of larger glaciers that formed the valleys in which they are now situated.

Q. True or false: Glaciers always travel downhill.
A. True. Glaciers are beholden to the powers of gravity. However, glacial retreat makes it appear that glaciers are

actually moving in the opposite direction. Glacial retreat is the melting of a glacier at its bottommost point. While the glacier is still moving downhill, it melts more quickly than its slow downhill movement, making it appear that it is actually moving up the face of a mountain.

Q. Glacier Gorge, Loch Vale, Chaos Canyon, Glacier Basin and Forest Canyon were all carved by what kind of glacier?
a) Valley glaciers   b) Cirque glaciers   c) Continental ice sheets
A. a) Valley glaciers. Though no valley glaciers exist in the park today, each of these geological areas owes its creation to these slow-moving behemoths.

---

*Elevations in Rocky Mountain National Park range from
7,500 to higher than 14,259 feet.*

Q. How many mountain peaks in the park top the 12,000-foot mark?

a) 12   b) 42   c) 74

A. c) 74. While a number of Rocky Mountain states may also have a fair number of peaks higher than 12,000 feet, Colorado is considered to have the greatest overall number of high-altitude peaks, thanks in large part to its 54 mountains that top the 14,000 foot mark—more than any other state in the U.S.

Q. What portion of the park is found above timberline, which is the point above which trees will not grow (11,200 to 11,500 feet)?

a) About one-third   b) About one-half   c) About three-quarters

A. a) About one-third.

Q. How many square miles does Rocky Mountain National Park encompass?

a) 329 square miles   b) 416 square miles   c) 534 square miles

A. b) 416 square miles; that's roughly 265,800 acres. While this may seem like a lot of land, in regards to sheer size Rocky Mountain National Park sits squarely in the middle of the pack when compared to the nation's other national parks. At 13.2 million acres, Wrangell-St. Elias National Park and Preserve is by far the largest national park in the United States.

Q. What three ecological zones comprise Rocky Mountain National Park?

a) Desert, alpine, tundra   b) High-alpine, tundra, montane
c) Montane, subalpine, alpine

A. c) Montane, subalpine and alpine make up the three ecological zones of Rocky Mountain National Park.

Q. What is a "montane" ecological zone?

A. Montane ecosystems are relatively moist, cool upland slopes located below timberline and dominated by large coniferous trees.

Q. What is a "subalpine" ecological zone?

A. Subalpine ecosystems refer to high upland slopes found just below timberline.

The canyons east of the park were carved by water flowing from glaciers that melted at the end of the Ice Age.

Q. What is an "alpine" ecological zone?
A. Alpine ecological zones are composed of elevated slopes situated above timberline.

Q. Between what altitude range is the montane forest system found?
a) Between 2,000 and 5,500 feet   b) Between 5,500 and 9,000 feet
c) Between 9,000 and 11,500 feet
A. b) Between 5,500 and 9,000 feet.

Q. Between what altitude range is a subalpine forest found?
a) Between 2,000 and 5,500 feet   b) Between 5,500 and 9,000 feet
c) Between 9,000 and 11,500 feet
A. c) Between 9,000 and 11,500 feet.

Q. What is "scree"?
a) High, slender clouds   b) A type of flower   c) A field of boulders
A. c) A field of boulders. Scree is the term used to describe rock fields found along mountainsides. Scree fields are created when landslides occur on rocky slopes, like those found throughout the park.

Q. What is a moraine?
a) A type of geological feature   b) A species of animal
c) A plant species
A. a) A type of geological feature. A moraine is an accumulation of earth and stones carried by a glacier and deposited on the ground when the glacier melts. You can see lateral moraines (from the glacier's sides) on the south and north sides of Moraine Park, and a terminal moraine against the small Eagle Cliff mountain to the east.

Q. How many lakes are located in the park?
a) 24   b) 97   c) 147
A. c) Rocky Mountain National Park has 147 lakes.

Q. What's the largest lake in the park?
a) Arrowhead Lake   b) Lawn Lake   c) Chipmunk Lake
A. a) Arrowhead Lake. With 34.9 surface acres, Arrowhead is the

_____

The Continental Divide runs north-south through Rocky Mountain National Park, along the mountain crests.

largest lake in Rocky Mountain National Park, followed closely by Lake Nanita with 34 surface acres.

Q. What's the smallest lake in Rocky Mountain National Park?
a) Chipmunk Lake   b) Embryo Lake   c) Marigold Pond d) all of the above
A. d) With 0.1 surface acre apiece, Chipmunk Lake, Embryo Lake and Marigold Pond are all tied for the smallest lakes in the park. However, there are a number of other small lakes and ponds in the park, but they remain unnamed.

Marigold Pond

Q. True or false: Lake Granby, which shares a shoreline with Rocky Mountain National Park, is the largest natural body of water in Colorado.
A. True. With 539,758 acres of water storage, Lake Granby is the largest *natural* body of water, but Blue Mesa Reservoir, near Gunnison, Colorado, which holds 829,500 acres of water, is the largest overall body of water in Colorado—though it's man-made.

Q. Roughly how old are the oldest rocks in the park?
a) 1.7 billion years old   b) 4.3 billion years old
c) 2.5 million years old
A. a) Around 1.7 billion years old. Metamorphic rocks, namely schist and gneiss, were formed when the Earth's plates placed immense pressure on sea sediments. When this great sea receded, it revealed many of the park's geological features.

Q. What is a metamorphic rock?
a) Any rock that has changed its composition from being exposed to pressure and heat   b) Any highly reflective rock
c) A rock that can be used for multiple applications
A. a) A metamorphic rock is any rock that changes composition after being exposed to pressure and heat.

All the park's rocks are either igneous or metamorphic.

Q. What defines a schist rock?
a) A hard, non-flaking rock   b) A rock that can be split into thin layers   c) A sandy, unstable rock
A. b) A metamorphic rock that can be split into thin layers. These rocks contain significant amounts of mica, which aid in the rock's ability to be split.

Q. What is a gneiss rock?
a) A rock with a banded appearance   b) Any rock containing combustible minerals   c) A rock with high sulfur content
A. a) Gneiss is a metamorphic rock that has a banded appearance and is composed of a number of minerals, most notably quartz or feldspar.

Q. Rocky Mountain National Park has a number of stunning silver plume granite features. How were these granite deposits created?
a) Volcanic eruptions   b) Tectonic shift   c) Erosion
A. a) Volcanic eruptions. After the creation of metamorphic rocks 1.7 billion years ago, magma from the Earth's core poured up through fissures, mixing with schist and gneiss rocks, eventually cooling and forming the park's omnipresent granite. This all happened roughly 1.4 billion years ago—give or take an epoch.

Q. What do "The Keyhole," "The Trough," "The Narrows" and "The Homestretch" all have in common?
a) They are scenic pullouts along Trail Ridge Road.
b) They are campsites in the park.
c) They are names of trail sections on the hike to the summit of Longs Peak.
A. c) They are all section names of the hike up Longs Peak.

Q. What four qualities define an ecosystem?
a) Weather, plant life, animal life and climate
b) Elevation, plant life, climate and sun exposure
c) Elevation, soil content, climate and land forms
A. c) Elevation, soil content, climate and land forms.

Q. The Kawuneeche Valley is found on the west side of the national park. This natural feature funnels snowmelt and rainwater into

---

Fault lines—along which earthquakes occur—in Rocky Mountain National Park have been only generally traced, but not yet completely mapped.

the storied Colorado River. "Kawuneeche" is an Arapaho Indian word. What does it mean?
a) Rainwater   b) Coyote   c) Sunset
A. b) Coyote.

Q. Longs Peak was named for what man?
a) Explorer Stephen Long
b) Cartographer Jonathon Long
c) Naturalist Edward Longs
A. a) Explorer Stephen Long. Long's party traveled west through the Great Plains in the early 1800s. They first caught sight of the Rocky Mountains in late June of 1820. Captain John R. Bell noted that day in his journal by writing, "The range had a beautiful and sublime appearance to us, after having been so long confined to the dull and uninteresting monotony of prairie country." This sentiment is still echoed by car-bound visitors driving west into the Rockies.

Longs Peak above Chasm Lake.

Q. Colorado's largest recorded earthquake is thought to have originated near the northern boundary of the park. In 1882, while seismic measurements were rudimentary, an earthquake of roughly a 6.6 magnitude shook the state. Do scientists believe this was a one-time phenomenon?
A. No. Seismologists guess that earthquakes of similar magnitude occur every 1,000 years, though smaller quakes most likely occur every 10 years.

Q. How many acres of designated wilderness are found in Rocky Mountain National Park?
a) 150,000   b) 175,000   c) 250,000
A. c) As of 2009, nearly 250,000 acres of the park's 265,000 acres

---

A wilderness designation means an area is set aside by law for preservation and protection of its natural condition.

are designated as wilderness—that's 94% of the park's entire area and enough space to fit almost 300 of New York City's Central Park.

Q. Prior to 2009, how many acres of Rocky Mountain National Park were designated as wilderness?
a) 1,492 acres   b) 2,917 acres   c) 3,370 acres
A. b) 2,917 acres. Today's nearly 250,000 acres of Rocky Mountain National Park wilderness owe their existence to Secretary of the Interior Ken Salazar—a former Colorado Congressman—who supported the Omnibus Public Lands Management Act of 2009, signed into law by President Barack Obama on March 30, of that year.

Q. How many acres of the United States are designated as wilderness?
a) 53.3 million   b) 109.5 million   c) 231.5 million
A. b) 109.5 million; that's about 5 million more acres than the area of the State of California.

Q. What percentage of America's total wilderness area does Rocky Mountain National Park provide?
a) 2.3 percent   b) 5.1 percent   c) 6.4 percent
A. a) With 109,505,482 acres of wilderness spread out over the entire U.S. and its territories, Rocky Mountain National Park's wilderness areas comprise roughly 2.3% of the nation's total.

Q. True or false: The high altitude of Rocky Mountain National Park's ecosystems make them less vulnerable to the negative effects of excess nitrogen than other parts of the country.
A. False. Rocky Mountain National Park's unique ecosystems actually make it more susceptible to excess nitrogen's harmful effects.

Q. What's a "riparian" area?
a) An area where water and land meet   b) A heavily forested area
c) The uppermost portion of a mountain
A. a) A riparian area is a specific   *Colorado riparian area amid pines.*

Riparian areas, also called "wetlands," can have standing water, or running water from small streams to large rivers.

type of habitat composed of both water and land; a marsh, or the edge of a lake or stream are examples of riparian habitats. Many park animals, including boreal toads and beavers, thrive in riparian habitats.

Q. How many miles of streams meander through Rocky Mountain National Park?
a) 450 miles   b) 500 miles   c) 550 miles
A. a) 450 miles. That's equivalent to a trip from Albuquerque, New Mexico, to Denver.

Q. How many mountain peaks within the park rise to the 10,000-foot mark?
a) 59   b) 114   c) 129
A. b) 114. While an impressive number, 10,000-foot peaks are considered relatively low-altitude affairs in Colorado, especially when you take into account the more than 500 mountains throughout the state that stand higher than 13,000 feet.

Although riparian areas cover only 2% of Colorado's land surface, they benefit 75% of the state's wildlife species.

WEATHER

Q. What is a "ground blizzard"?
a) A blizzard that originates in lower elevations, working its way up the mountain
b) The collapse of snow from a laden evergreen bough
c) White-out conditions that are caused by swirling snow blown up from the ground
A. c) Ground blizzards are white-out conditions that are caused by swirling snow blown up from the ground. Winds can be extremely high and gusty in the park, especially above tree line. It's important to be constantly cognizant of your location, especially during winter, to ensure you do not get lost.

Q. How low in temperature can a Rocky Mountain National Park wind-chill reach?
a) 0 degrees Fahrenheit   b) -50 degrees Fahrenheit
c) -100 degrees Fahrenheit
A. c) Wind-chill (which is a way of a describing temperature by taking into account the cooling effect of wind) can reach temperatures of -100 degrees Fahrenheit (-73 degrees Celsius) in the park.

Q. What three months of the year see the highest snowpack levels within the park?

a) January, February, March   b) December, January, February
c) October, November, December
A. a) Traditionally, the highest snowpack occurs in the months of January, February and March. High snowpack can obviously mean increased avalanche conditions; however, it also means exceptional cross-country skiing and snowshoeing opportunities. Heavy snow in the park is integral to the welfare of the state. Lots of snow means lots of water when the spring melt arrives. This water supports local communities throughout Colorado and every state downriver from the headwaters of the state's rivers, including the well-known Colorado River. The state's rafting companies are fairly keen on heavy snowpack conditions come springtime as well.

Q. Why is the water shut off at winter campsites?
A. As with any cold-weather location, water easily freezes in pipes, often causing them to burst. So if you're camping in the park during winter, don't expect full campsite hookups.

Q. Generally, between what months are best to attempt a hike up Longs Peak?
a) March to June   b) June to August   c) July to September
A. c) Mid-July to mid-September doesn't guarantee optimal hiking conditions, but they offer the best bet for good-weather travel to the top.

Q. True or false: Climate and weather mean different things.
A. True. Climate refers to an area's long-term weather patterns, while weather indicates the short-term elements of a climate.

Q. What geographical feature in the park divides it into two weather and climate patterns?
a) Lake Granby   b) the Continental Divide   c) Longs Peak
A. b) The Continental Divide, which controls weather patterns due to its size and ability to shape the wind and moisture flow of the clouds.

Fewer than 5% of Rocky Mountain National Park visitors experience the park in the winter. Fully 95% of all visitors come in the spring, summer or fall.

Q. Generally, what weather and climate patterns distinguish the east and west portions of Rocky Mountain National Park?
a) The eastern side is usually drier.
b) The western side is usually drier.
c) There is no distinguishable difference between park areas.
A. a) The eastern part of the park is usually drier than that of the west. East Rocky Mountain National Park sees, on average, 13 inches of precipitation, while the wetter west side tallies 20 inches annually.

Q. Spring conditions in the park usually begin in the montane elevations (8,000-9,500 feet) in late April. How many more months will it take for the same conditions to reach the subalpine elevations (9,500-11,500 feet)?
a) 1 month   b) 1.5 months   c) 2 months
A. c) Two months. Spring conditions don't reach these higher elevations until June—a summer month for much of the rest of the continent.

Q. Typically, what is the coldest month in the park?
a) November   b) December   c) January
A. c) January. Even daytime temperatures in January are often less than 20 degrees F.

Q. In which month does it never snow in the park?
a) July   b) August   c) It can snow at any time.
A. c) It can snow at any time. Because the Rocky Mountains create their own weather patterns, snow is always a possibility, no matter the time of year.

Q. What is usually the warmest month in the park?
a) June   b) July   c) August
A. b) July. Temperatures in the park can reach the mid-80s.

Q. Did you know there are three very common forms of frozen water that occur in the park? Can you name them?
a) Snow, sleet, graupel   b) Snow, sleet, hail
c) Rime, glaze ice, snow
A. c) Rime, glaze ice and snow.

Thinner mountain air in the park means that ultraviolet exposure is greater than at lower elevations.

Q. How does the National Weather Service define "rime"?
A. The National Weather Service defines rime as composed of tiny balls of ice that form when tiny drops of water freeze on contact with the surface.

Q. How does the National Weather Service define "glaze ice"?
A. According to the National Weather Service, glaze ice is "a layer or coating of ice that is generally smooth and clear, and forms on exposed objects by freezing of liquid raindrops."

Q. Thanks to grade school cutouts, we all know what a basic snowflake looks like, but exactly how many points does a true snowflake have?
a) Four   b) Six   c) Eight
A. b) Six.

Q. What mathematical concept explains the unique and intricate pattern of snowflakes?
a) Absolute Zero   b) Fractals   c) Pi
A. Fractals. For the non-mathematically inclined, a fractal is a geometric figure that repeats itself under several levels of magnification. If that's the case, the physical shape of an item, like a snowflake, repeats itself nearly infinitesimally.

Q. How many snowfall monitoring stations does Rocky Mountain National Park have?
a) None   b) Six   c) Ten
A. b) Six. They are located in Willow Park, Bear Lake, Copeland Lake, Lake Irene, Phantom Valley and Ouzel Falls.

Cold Weather Tip
Cold weather, like that of a Rocky Mountain National Park winter, can quickly suck the energy out of digital devices. Keep cameras and phones warm to extend their battery life. If you're outdoors, be sure to secure your electronic device in an internal pocket to keep it warm and in service.

Scientists believe that microscopic organisms and dust particles land in the park after being picked up along wind streams originating from as far away as China.

Q. On clear days in the park, how far out into the horizon can you clearly see?
a) 75 miles   b) 100 miles   c) 150 miles
A. b) On clear days, when haze is low and conditions are just right (usually during winter), clear views can be had of landmarks nearly 100 miles away.

Wild Sculptures
Did you know that the wind sculpts trees in the park? Exposed trees in windy areas often have limbs growing only to one side. These oddly shaped trees use their trunks to protect their needles and leaves from being torn off by high winds. Trees with this feature make it easy to tell the history of wind direction and force within the park.

Q. Wind studies in Rocky Mountain National Park in the 1970s and 1980s recorded impressive gusts atop Longs Peak. Up to how many miles an hour did these record gusts reach?
a) Up to 100 miles an hour   b) Up to 200 miles an hour
c) Up to 250 miles an hour
A. b) Up to 200 miles an hour. Average wind guts on Longs Peak reach around 65 miles an hour. Winter wind speeds at the Alpine Visitor Center averaged 48 miles an hour, with occasional gusts reaching near 80 miles an hour. Summer winds throughout the park are typically much more subdued.

Q. If you find yourself atop Longs Peak in the winter, what are your chances of experiencing wind gusts that exceed 100 mph?
a) 1 in 7   b) 1 in 5   c) 1 in 2
A. b) 1 in 5. According to winter wind studies done at the apex of Longs Peak, one out of every five days on this 14,259-foot peak sees gusts stronger than 100 mph.

Snow around the Alpine Visitor Center insulates the building, when it's closed for the winter, keeping the indoor temperature about 20 degrees F.

Q. You may hear someone in the park refer to chinooks. What are they talking about?
a) Wind   b) Fish   c) Water flow
A. a) Wind. A chinook is a warm wind in winter that can raise park temperatures by as much as 50 degrees F. But why "chinook"? The air masses that cause this type of wind originates in the Pacific Northwest, where the word means "snow eater" in one of the local languages.

Q. What is a bora wind?
a) Warm, wet winds that run along river basins
b) Slight breezes that are constant in the park
c) Cold, dry winds that descend mountaintops
A. c) Bora winds are cold, dry walls of wind that descend mountains. Bora wind gusts commonly reach speeds of 50-60 mph.

A chinook wind can raise the temperature from "winter" to "spring" within a few hours.

ANIMALS

Mammals

Q. What month is best to see newborn animals in the park?
a) April   b) May   c) June
A. c) June. This early summer month is your best bet for seeing coyote pups, deer and moose calves, mule deer fawns and young cottontail rabbits.

Q. How many individual mammalian species are found within Rocky Mountain National Park?
a) 50   b) 60   c) 70
A. b) In all, 60 kinds of mammals are found within Rocky Mountain National Park, and that's not including tourists. Statewide, nearly 750 species of animals call Colorado home.

Q. True or false: Feeding wildlife within the park helps the animals survive their harsh environment.
A. Absolutely false. Feeding wildlife is never a good idea. Not only can animals be dangerous up close, but feeding wild creatures teaches them to rely on humans for sustenance. Animals that get food from humans tend to lose their natural hunting and foraging abilities, making it hard for them to survive in the wild. Also, while food may be ample for hand-fed animals during the

park's peak visitor seasons, the colder, harsher months show a relative dearth of vacationers, meaning these otherwise human-dependent animals have a lesser chance of finding food, hurting their chances for survival. Furthermore, the hand-outs that visitors usually offer wild animals are not part of their natural diet and may be detrimental to their health.

Q. Hibernating animals that have come to rely on human food often don't survive their annual hibernations. Why not?

A. Even if before hibernation an animal gains the usual amount of weight by eating human handouts instead of foraged food, their quality of stored fat isn't as high, meaning the human-food–dependant animal would have less of an ability to sustain long periods of inactivity.

Q. What does it mean when a ranger says an animal has been "extirpated" from the park?
a) Its population has grown beyond park boundaries.
b) It no longer exists within the park.
c) It has been purposely removed from the park.

A. b) Extirpated means a once-native animal no longer exists within a certain location, though it can still be found in other areas in the world. Wolves and leopard frogs are examples of extirpated animals from Rocky Mountain National Park.

Q. True or false: Some animals in the park may actually carry the bubonic plague, the same "black death" that ravaged medieval Europe.

A. True. Partially because of the ever-prevalent threat of diseases, park rangers advise you do not come into physical contact with any of the park's animals. Thanks to this good stewardship, no one in the park has ever been infected with this disease.

Q. What type of bear, though rarely seen, resides in Rocky Mountain National Park?
a) Black bear   b) Brown bear   c) Sun bear

A. a) Black bear are native residents of the Rocky Mountain National Park region. Though they're secretive and not often seen by visitors, there is a healthy black bear population within the park.

The Chow Busters are a group of park volunteers whose job it is to ensure park visitors refrain from actively or accidentally feeding wildlife.

Q. How many black bears are thought to reside in Rocky Mountain National Park?
a) 30 to 50   b) 50 to 60   c) 60 to 70
A. a) Rangers estimate the black bear population in Rocky Mountain National Park to be between 30 and 50 animals. According to park officials, there is really no way to know how many black bears were present in the area prior to the park's creation. Most people did not believe it was important to monitor black bear populations prior to the early 1900s. Researchers study-

ing black bears in the early 2000s speculated that there might have been even fewer black bears in the park historically because of the lack of natural foods and high-quality habitat that exist within the park.

Q. True or false: Grizzly bears are found in the park.
A. False. Officially, there are no known grizzly bears anywhere in Colorado—the last bear was likely killed soon after the park's creation. Though they once were native to the state, excessive hunting, trapping and poisoning of these bears resulted in their eventual statewide extinction. While the Colorado Division of Wildlife has declared Colorado a grizzly-bear-free state, a few locals in the southern section of Colorado swear there are still a handful of these forest giants roaming untouched areas of nearly inaccessible Colorado.

Q. Though rare, encounters with bears do occur. To better insure a bear interaction doesn't end poorly, what should you do?
a) Yell loudly and authoritatively at the bear.
b) Run from the bear.
c) Stand still or back away slowly until the bear leaves on its own.
A. c) If you encounter a bear, don't panic. Stand still or slowly back away from the bear until it leaves. If the bear does not leave in a few minutes, continue to back away until you are at a safe distance and then continue on in the opposite direction of the bear.

Though once prolific in the area, by 1920 overzealous hunting had led to the absence of grizzly bears in Rocky Mountain National Park.

Q. What is the average weight of adult black bears in Rocky Mountain National Park?
a) 175 pounds   b) 210 pounds   c) 350 pounds
A. a) Adult male black bears in the park weigh on average 175 pounds, while females weigh in at 121 pounds. If these numbers sound a bit low for full-grown bears, they are. In fact, black bears in the park are 30 to 50 percent smaller than their counterparts in western Colorado.

Q. In general, how old is a female black bear outside of Rocky Mountain National Park when she has her first cub?
a) Between three and four years old
b) Between five and six years old
c) Between seven and eight years old
A. b) Between five and six years of age.

> The taste and temptation of human food to bears is so strong that even the less-than-lethal sting of rubber riot bullets aren't enough to permanently deter a scavenging, human-food addicted bear from attempting to feed on people-provided meals.

Q. Why are there believed to be so few black bears in the park as compared to other locations, and why are they so often found to weigh much less than nearby populations?
a) The park's black bear population is actually a bear sub-species.
b) The habitat is poor for black bears.
c) The area is over-hunted.
A. b) Rocky Mountain National Park is actually a fairly poor habitat for black bears. In fact, it's believed that one of the main reasons bears are found in the park at all is that hunting within park boundaries is illegal.

Q. True or false: The beaver is mostly nocturnal.
A. True. "Busy as a beaver" is a common colloquialism, but most people don't know they're also "night owls."

Q. What color are beaver teeth?
a) White   b) Orange   c) Brown

Black bear densities in Rocky Mountain National Park are estimated at one-sixth less than other Colorado areas, and up to one-twelfth as dense as bear populations in other Rocky Mountain states.

A. b) Orange. The orange color comes from the hard enamel covering this rodent's incisors. Color is not the only odd feature of beaver teeth. In addition to having hard, orange incisors, they are also self-sharpening, ensuring that the more they use their teeth the sharper they get—a helpful feat when your livelihood depends on gnawing through trees.

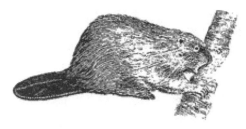

Q. What do you call a baby beaver?
a) A pup   b) A cub   c) A kit
A. c) A kit.

Q. Can you name six animals that commonly prey upon beavers in the park?
A. Coyotes, wolverines, bears, hawks, owls and eagles.

Q. How many beaver colonies are thought to be in Rocky Mountain National Park?
a) Fewer than 5   b) Between 15 and 20   c) More than 20
A. b) Between 15 and 20.

Q. Are beaver numbers in Rocky Mountain National Park increasing or decreasing?
A. They are decreasing. The causes of this decline are still not fully understood.

Q. Beavers store large amounts of wood in their lodges for food in the winter. What two types of trees do they most commonly hoard?
a) Ponderosa pine and Douglas-fir   b) Willow and aspen
c) Dogwood and lodgepole pine
A. b) Willow and aspen. It's not uncommon for a few cuttings to survive the beaver's efforts and sprout new growths from the walls of the dam they've built. In fact, the industrious beaver increases the health and dramatically changes its ecosystem. Its foraging and tree-cutting serve to create new riparian environments for a host of animals, and allow new growth in trees to come in thicker and hardier at the site of their cuttings.

Due to the abundance of small rodents in the park, combined with humans illegally feeding animals, coyotes in Rocky Mountain National Park grow very large. Visitors often mistake them for wolves.

Q. How many baby beavers are born to mating pairs in a season?
a) Just one   b) Between two and three   c) Between four and five
A. b) Between two and three.

Q. Beavers are considered keystone species. What does it mean to be a keystone species?
a) They significantly impact their environment.
b) They are at the bottom of the food chain.
c) They are at the top of the food chain.
A. a) All keystone species affect their environment in a very significant and measurable way. The changes they make to their habitat lead to the appearance of other, diverse species. The beaver's forest clearing and dam building firmly establish these animals as keystone species, upon which other animals rely. When beavers dam a river with their lodges, they create marshes, wetlands and lakes, where a diversity of animals thrive. In addition, while their tree-cutting initially turns forests into glens, their pruning actually allows for healthier forests to emerge with greater abundance and stronger root structures when new growth begins.

Q. Which species of deer, common in the United States, is larger: white-tailed deer or mule deer?
A. Mule deer. A fully grown mule deer buck can weigh 500 pounds, while a white-tailed deer tops the scales at 300 pounds. When traveling through Rocky Mountain National Park, be on the lookout for mule deer, the most common variety throughout Colorado.

Mule deer buck (left) with antlers, and doe using her "mule-sized" ears to check out a human.

Herbivores (plant eaters) are of two types: browsers, like mule deer, eat grasses and woody vegetation; grazers, including elk, eat grasses unless winter scarcity makes them eat twigs and bark.

Q. How do mule deer get their name?
a) They were once used as pack animals   b) From the shape of their ears   c) From the braying sound they make
A. b) Their name comes from their large mule-like ears.

Q. Park rangers have found mule deer skeletons high up in trees. How do they think they got there?
a) Mule deer can climb.   b) A predator placed it there.
c) A poacher left it there.
A. b) The treed deer was most likely placed there by a mountain lion. After a mountain lion eats its fill, it will often hide the rest of its meal, sometimes even in the boughs of a tree.

Q. Why are deer in Rocky Mountain National Park outfitted with tracking collars?
a) To track migration patterns   b) To locate deer for disease testing   c) To follow population numbers
A. b) Tracking collars are used in mule deer populations within the park to locate animals for intermittent tests needed to search for Chronic Wasting Disease.

Q. Scientists frequently tranquilize deer in the park for research purposes. How long does it take for the tranquilizer they use to take down a fully grown mule deer?
a) 5 minutes   b) 10 minutes   c) 15 minutes
A. b) 10 minutes. If you're familiar with the speed of a fully grown deer, you know they can cover quite a bit of ground in 10 minutes. Researchers need to be ready for a hike once the dart hits its mark.

The tranquilizing drug used by scientists to incapacitate mule deer in the park does not render the animals unconscious. Instead, the tranquilizer keeps the mule deer from moving; the animal still has control of its hearing and sight. The drug used to tranquilize deer in the park requires a second drug—administered by researchers—to undo the effects.

Deer see color differently than humans do. Instead of orange and red, they see shades of gray. This slight colorblindness helps hunters stay camouflaged from their prey but visible to fellow hunters.

Q. On average, how long does it take park scientists to tranquilize, test, tag and reanimate a mule deer?
a) 15 minutes   b) 30 minutes   c) 45 minutes
A. c) About 45 minutes.

Q. How many elk reside in the park?
a) 1,000   b) 3,000   c) There are no elk in Rocky Mountain National Park.
A. b) It is thought roughly 3,000 elk live in Rocky Mountain National Park. Luckily for the elk here, their home is a no-hunting location. Statewide, hunters in Colorado harvest anywhere from 40,000 to 50,000 elk in a single season—that's the largest amount of any state.

Q. In the fall and winter months, where are you more likely to see elk in the park?
a) At higher elevations.   b) At lower elevations.
c) Equally spread throughout the park.
A. b) At lower elevations. When the colder months come to Rocky Mountain National Park, the park's elk residents descend to lower elevations to escape the colder conditions found higher up. Food is scarce during the winter, and elk have a better chance of successfully foraging at these lower elevations.

Q. What does it mean to say the elk are "in rut"?
a) The males are losing their antlers.   b) It is mating season.
c) It is calving season.
A. b) The rut is a time of year, usually in the fall, when elk begin to mate. Mating elk are very active and the bugles of the bulls can be heard echoing throughout the forests.

Q. So you want to hear the shrill bugle of a bull elk. What time of year should you visit to increase your odds of hearing an elk call?
a) Fall   b) Winter   c) Spring
A. a) Fall. During fall, elk begin their mating season. To attract females, bulls bellow a shrill bugle to attract females. An elk's bugle can be heard for dozens of miles throughout the park. As with any wild animal, be sure to give elk lots of space during the rut, because they can be overly aggressive at this time of year. In

---

Hunters sometimes refer to "the wily wapiti." When they do so, their last word is a Native American word for "elk."

fact, parts of Rocky Mountain National Park are completely closed to visitor traffic during fall in order to better ensure a successful elk mating season.

Q. What does it mean for elk to "yard up?"
a) They are fighting.   b) They are growing antlers.   c) They are gathering.
A. When herds of elk congregate in lower-elevation open grazing areas, most often in winter months, they are said to "yard up."

Q. What is a bull elk's group of mating females called?
a) A harem   b) A herd   c) A flock
A. a) A harem. A single bull elk can claim a harem of up to 60 cows and will fight would-be usurpers to keep them.

Q. The park employs a number of mules and horses for summer work to assist rangers in their duties. Since winters are too cold to stable livestock, where are these hard-working animals wintered?
a) Grand Canyon National Park in Arizona
b) Fort Laramie National Historic Site in Wyoming
c) Gila National Forest in New Mexico
A. b) Fort Laramie National Historic Site in Wyoming.

Q. What is a marmot?
a) A type of bird   b) A type of amphibian   c) A type of rodent
A. c) The largest of the park's squirrely species, the marmot is a rodent that lives among rocky outcroppings and measures between 19 and 26 inches.

Q. During winter hibernation in the park, how much body weight can resident marmots lose?
a) A quarter of their body weight   b) Half their body weight
c) Three-quarters of their body weight
A. b) Yellow-bellied marmots can lose up to half their body weight during hibernation.

Hibernaculum, *the Latin term for a winter tent, is the word scientists use for an animal's hibernation location.*

Q. While hibernating, park marmots can drop their body temperatures to what temperature?
a) 60 degrees F   b) 50 degrees F   c) 40 degrees F
A. c) 40 degrees F, just 8 degrees above freezing.

Q. During hibernation, yellow-bellied marmots slow down their breathing. How often do they take a breath while in hibernation?
a) Once every one to three minutes   b) Once every three to six minutes   c) Once every ten minutes
A. b) While in hibernation, the park's yellow-bellied marmots breathe once every three to six minutes, and their heartbeat drops to one beat per minute.

Q. Yellow-bellied marmots begin to hibernate between September and October in the park. When do they emerge from their winter respites?
a) Between March and April   b) Between April and May
c) Between May and June
A. b) Between April and May.

Q. True or false: Moose can be seen in the park.
A. True. Though not a common sight, these hulking riparian herbivores can be seen near the park's many lakes. If you're dead set on seeing a moose, your best bet is to visit the Kawuneeche Valley, where the majority of moose sightings occur.

Q. In what year did the Colorado Division of Wildlife begin introducing moose into nearby North Park, Colorado?
a) 1978   b) 1983   c) 2006
A. a) 1978. Since their introduction by the Colorado Division of Wildlife from the Uinta Mountains and the Grand Tetons in Wyoming, moose have found their way into Rocky Mountain National Park from nearby North Park, most commonly in order to calve their young.

Dawn and dusk are the best times for wildlife viewing because that's when the animals are most active.

Q. What animal is the largest member of the deer family?
a) Mule deer   b) Elk   c) Moose
A. c) Moose. Tipping the scales at 1,800 pounds and seven feet tall, a fully grown bull moose is easily the largest member of the deer family. While not abundant, there is a moose population present in Rocky Mountain National Park. Statewide, there are thought to be roughly 1,000 moose in Colorado, mostly located near Rocky Mountain National Park.

Q. True or false: Moose are strong swimmers.
A. True. Even with an average weight of 1,800 pounds, moose are exceptional swimmers. In fact, it isn't uncommon to see moose dive beneath the water's surface for food.

Q. What do a mountain lion, cougar, catamount and puma all have in common?
A. They are all names for the same animal. Mountain lions in and around Rocky Mountain National Park range in size from 80 to 180 pounds. This often misunderstood and too-often-feared big cat is known by a variety of names. If you encounter a mountain lion—North America's largest feline—play it cool. Back away slowly, being sure to never turn your back, and make yourself look as large as possible. Be sure to keep pets and small children close by.

While the park does not have an actual research count on the number of mountain lions here due to the difficulty of tracking these stealthy cats, they assume the park has a healthy mountain lion population. The only documented incident of a lion attacking a human was in 1997, when a 10-year-old boy was running a few minutes ahead of his family along the North Inlet Trail on the west side. Unfortunately, the boy later died from injuries he sustained in the attack.

Q. How many species of rodents are found in Rocky Mountain National Park?
a) 12   b) 23   c) 42
A. b) 23 species of rodents live within the park.

---

*Cougars often climb trees overhanging known game trails
and wait until an animal passes by, then drop down
atop the animal to take it by surprise.*

Q. How many species of squirrel are found in the park?
a) Three   b) Seven   c) Nine
A. c) Nine species of squirrel can be found in the park.

Q. How many rat and mice species are found in the park?
a) Three   b) Six   c) Ten
A. c) There are ten species of mice and rats living inside the park.

Q. True or false: The beaver and the porcupine are both rodents.
A. True.

Q. What type of mammal is the most abundant in Rocky Mountain National Park?
a) Rodents   b) Ungulates   c) Marsupials
A. a) Rodents. This isn't surprising when you take into account the fact that rodents make up roughly 40% of the world's known mammalian species.

Q. By what other name are "rock rabbits" and "coneys" known
a) Pika   b) Yellow-bellied marmot   c) Boreal toad
A. Pika. These small, furry rodents are very common in the park's tundra.

Q. What is a "haystack" and what does it have to do with a pika's survival?
a) It's a secondary home
b) It's a nesting area
c) It's a type of food storage
A. c) A pika's haystack is made up of edible grasses and is used as a food cache put away for winter months. Some haystacks are quite large, taking up the same volume as a full-sized refrigerator.

Q. True or false: Pikas used stored food as their main source of sustenance during the winter.
A. False. While pikas do store large amounts of food, they still actively forage during the winter, using their large reserves as emergency stashes.

Rodents are defined, in part, by their large incisor teeth, which are made exclusively for gnawing.

Q. When was the first recorded sighting of pronghorn (a cousin of the antelope and very common on the Great Plains) within the park?
a) 1919   b) 1947   c) 2005
A. c) 2005. Prior to 2005, pronghorn, though exceptionally abundant a few hundred miles east of the park, had never been

observed within park boundaries. It's thought that the drought conditions of the early 2000s may have led this park stranger farther out of its usual habitat in search of better grazing. Sightings in the 21st century have included 2002, 2003 and 2005 in

Kawuneeche Valley below the Never Summer Mountains

the Kawuneeche Valley. As of this printing there have not been any sightings since 2005.

Q. What is a "chickaree"?
a) A type of squirrel.   b) A type of bird   c) A species of lizard
A. a) A chickaree is a squirrel often found throughout Rocky Mountain National Park, especially in rocky outcroppings and near campgrounds, scrounging for leftovers. Weighing about half a pound, these bushy-tailed scavengers show little fear of humans, often taunting hikers with their high-pitched calls.

Q. What do red squirrels, Douglas squirrels, pine squirrels and chickarees have in common?
a) None of them is found outside of Colorado.
b) They are all names for the same animal.
c) They each migrate south from Canada.
A. b) They are all names for the same animal, common in Rocky Mountain National Park.

Q. Abert's squirrels call Rocky Mountain National Park home. In what specific type of tree will these tiny mammals reside?

In winter, snow-white ptarmigans are best seen near Trail Ridge Road, beyond the winter gate at Rainbow Curve.

a) Mature ponderosa pines   b) Juvenile Norfolk pines
c) Well-established aspen groves
A. a) Abert's squirrels, which got their name from J.J. Abert—a naturalist from the 1800s—make their home in mature ponderosa pines.

Q. Left on their own, how old do the park's Abert's squirrels get?
a) Between two and three years old
b) Between five and six years old
c) Between seven and eight years old
A. c) Between seven and eight years old.

Q. How can you tell an Abert's squirrel from other squirrels in the park?
a) By the sounds they make
b) By the shape of their tails
c) By their ear hair
A. c) Abert's squirrels have distinctive white tufts of fur growing from their ears. These furry flags are most noticeable in winter.

Q. Abert's squirrels do not hibernate, nor do they hide food for leaner months. What other park squirrel shares this characteristic?
a) No other park squirrel shares this characteristic.
b) Ground squirrels   c) Rock squirrels
A. a) No other park squirrel shares this characteristic. Abert's squirrels are the only squirrel in the park not to "squirrel away" food. This lifestyle means they must be active all year to survive, even in the harshest winters. In all, there are 18 squirrel species scurrying around Rocky Mountain National Park, and all but the Abert's squirrel hide food for the winter. The other squirrel species in the park range from the tiny lesser chipmunk to the burrowing Wyoming ground squirrel.

Q. The ponderosa pine, a favorite home of Abert's squirrels, does more than provide shelter; it's also their main source of food. On what part of the tree do Abert's squirrels feed?
a) The needles   b) The cones   c) The seeds   d) all of these

---

Snowshoe hare babies are born with full fur and with their eyes open; they grow to adult size in only three to five months.

A. d) All of these. Abert's squirrels eat ponderosa pine needles, seeds, buds and cones.

Q. Besides pine, what else will Abert's squirrels eat?
a) Insects   b) Dead animals   c) Mistletoe   d) All of these
A. d) All of these. When given the opportunity, these omnivorous squirrels will eat fungi, mistletoe, insects, dead animals, and even antlers and bone.

Q. What animal, often seen in the park, is also the Colorado state mammal?
a) Mountain goat   b) Elk   c) Bighorn sheep
A. c) Bighorn sheep, often seen scaling nearly-sheer cliffs, are Rocky Mountain National Park residents and the state mammal.

Q. True or false: Like the rings on a tree, you can tell the age of a bighorn sheep by the rings on its horns.
A. True. For each year a male bighorn sheep is alive, he grows another horn length, which is identified by a visible ring where growth occurs.

Bighorn sheep are very easily stressed by human interaction. In fact, the psychological stress from an encounter with a park visitor can cause the animal to become sick and die.

Q. What is said to have been the most prevalent cause of the population decline of bighorn sheep well into the 1950s?

a) Disease   b) Over-hunting
c) Domestic sheep
A. c) The most devastating threat to bighorn sheep in the area came from domesticated sheep. This farm animal spread diseases through the wild bighorn population and competed for the same food source. At their lowest population level in the

When bighorn males fight during the mating ritual, they charge at each other at about 40 mph, and the resulting horn-to-horn collisions can be heard a mile away.

1950s, it's thought that only 150 wild bighorn sheep roamed the park, down from its original population that ranged in thousands. Thanks to programs set in place by rangers and other environmentalists, including the closure of neighboring sheep farms, the bighorn sheep population is again well represented within the park, with about 600 thought to reside inside park boundaries.

Q. What is the Bighorn Brigade?
a) A volunteer group   b) A group of researchers   c) A hunting club
A. a) The Bighorn Brigade is a group of volunteers whose job is to educate the public about the park's bighorn sheep population, and to act as crossing guards, holding traffic at bay when the Colorado state mammal crosses Fall River Road—a common throughway for this ungulate.

Q. What's an ermine?
a) A short-tailed weasel   b) A marmot   c) A ptarmigan
A. a) Ermine is another name for the short-tailed weasel.

Q. Are ptarmigans and short-tailed weasels—two animals that turn white in the winter—considered albinos?
A. No. Animals that change white in the winter do so by purposely growing white fur or feathers. Albino animals are white because they lack melanin, the compound that produces color. True albinos will even lack eye color, displaying pink irises.

Q. How many wolves are thought to inhabit Rocky Mountain National Park?
a) There are no wolves in Rocky Mountain National Park.
b) 1-20   c) 21-40
A. a) While once common in the area, wolves are no longer found here. In fact, wolves were likely gone before the park was established. Hunting, trapping, poison and development were the main causes of wolf extirpation in the area now encompassed by Rocky Mountain National Park.

If you're in the park during winter and are very, very lucky, you might experience a rare sighting of an ermine around Lily Lake or Sprague Lake, but their white fur makes them very hard to see.

Birds

Q. How many bird species reside in Rocky Mountain National Park?
a) 150   b) 280   c) More than 280
A. c) More than 280 bird species are found in Rocky Mountain National Park, making it a haven not only for avian animals, but also for bird watchers. When in the park, look for the Colorado state bird, the lark bunting. The state as a whole is home to more than 460 bird species.

Q. What three types of bluebirds can commonly be seen in Rocky Mountain National Park? Hint: Two of the three take their names from a compass point.
a) Mountain bluebirds, western bluebirds and eastern bluebirds
b) Lake bluebirds, northern bluebirds and southern bluebirds
c) White-tailed bluebirds, western bluebirds and northern bluebirds
A. a) Mountain bluebirds, western bluebirds and eastern bluebirds.

Q. Generally, when do the ubiquitous mountain bluebirds return to the park after winter absences?
a) March   b) April   c) May
A. a) Mid-March.

Q. Approximately what month do golden eagle chicks hatch in the park?
a) March   b) April   c) May
A. c) May. Most eagle pairs lay two eggs a season, though often only one chick survives to adulthood.

Q. Which eagle species is larger: the golden eagle or the bald eagle?
A. With a wingspan of up to 7.5 feet, the golden eagle is, on average, the larger of the two.

Q. Roughly how many mating golden eagle pairs are thought to reside in Rocky Mountain National Park
a) 5 mating pairs   b) 7 mating pairs   c) 10 mating pairs
A. c) 10 mating pairs.

Climbing routes in Rocky Mountain National Park may be closed to protect raptors like eagles, falcons, and owls during their courtship and parenting seasons.

Q. How many different mates will a golden eagle have in a lifetime
a) One   b) Five   c) We don't know.
A. a) One. Golden eagles are extraordinarily faithful animals. They'll only take another mate if their original partner passes away.

Q. What is an eagle aerie?
a) An egg   b) A hunting ground   c) A nest
A. c) A nest. Eagle aeries are made up of large sticks wedged into rock ledges and trees.

Q. Returning from winter migrations, which sex of golden eagle is seen in the park first, males or females?
A. Male golden eagles tend to arrive at nesting sites first, followed some days later by their mate. The male arrives early to scout out new or existing nesting sites for that year's mating season.

It's common for an eagle pair to have more than one nest site at any given time. Mating pairs may switch nests every year or they may never change locations in their lifetime. Scientists believe eagles keep up multiple properties to confuse would-be predators or to escape parasites.

Q. Generally, how many eggs does a golden eagle lay in a season?
a) One   b) Two   c) Three
A. b) Two. Eagle eggs are off-white with darker splotches speckled throughout the shell. Though two chicks are hatched, usually only one survives. One chick usually out-competes the other for attention and food. The dominant chick has been known to physically kick its sibling over the side of the nest, effectively killing that bird and ensuring that it receives the most to eat. Talk about survival of the fittest!

Q. What park animal does not turn white in winter?
a) Ptarmigans   b) Snowshoe hares   c) Golden eagles
A. c) Golden eagles, which stay brown all year long.

The peregrine falcon is the fastest animal in the world. In a steep dive, it has been clocked at upwards of 200 mph. This falcon uses its dive speed to descend upon its prey of other birds, colliding with them in mid-air.

Q. The peregrine falcon, a park resident, was once nearly driven to extinction due to what?
A. DDT. This once-common pesticide, now banned from use, was linked to the peregrine falcons' near demise—as well as the near collapse of many other avian species. DDT caused the shells of bird eggs to be abnormally thin, which meant eggs easily broke before chicks hatched. Since its use was outlawed, the peregrine falcon population has made a tremendous recovery, and was removed from the endangered species list in 1999. Look near the park's border with Grand Lake or Estes Park for these predator birds.

Q. What is the most common hawk seen in Rocky Mountain National Park?
a) Red-tailed hawk   b) Buteo hawk   c) Broad-winged hawk
A. a) The red-tailed hawk. In fact, this hawk species is the most common in all of North America and has a wide dispersal over the Western Hemisphere. The first scientifically studied red-tailed hawk was from Jamaica.

It is an undeniably capable hunter of small rodents. Look for the hawk at the edge of open fields and perched upon fence posts and telephone poles scanning its surroundings for a meal.

Q. What hawk, common to the park, is the largest of its species?
a) Broad-winged hawk   b) Buteo hawk   c) Red-tailed hawk
A. c) The red-tailed hawk. With a wingspan of up to two feet and weighing in at slightly more than three pounds, the red-tailed hawk is still no bigger than a mallard.

Q. Which raptor is a park visitor most likely to see: a hawk, eagle or owl?
a) Eagle   b) Owl   c) Hawk
A. c) A hawk, more specifically, a red-tailed hawk.

A female red-tailed hawk is about 30% larger than a male.

Q. How many times more powerful is the eyesight of a red-tailed hawk than yours or mine?
a) Eight times   b) Ten times   c) Twenty times
A. a) Assuming you have perfect 20/20 vision, a red-tailed hawk's eyesight is eight times more powerful than a human's. If you had the eyesight of a hawk, you'd be able to read your favorite novel while standing in the end zone of a football field while the book was placed on the 20-yard line.

Q. True or false: A pair of red-tailed hawks mate for life.
A. True.

Q. Under ideal conditions, how long can a red-tailed hawk live?
a) 5 years   b) 10 years   c) 20 years
A. c) Up to 20 years.

Q. In what ecological zone in the park are red-tailed hawk nests most commonly found?
a) Montane   b) Tundra   c) Alpine
A. a) In the montane zone, an ecological area found between 5,600 and 9,500 feet above sea level.

Q. The broad-tailed hummingbird is a familiar summer sight in Rocky Mountain National Park. When winter approaches, this tiny flyer migrates south. Where does this bird spend its winter months?
a) In Mexico and Central America   b) In South America
c) In the southwestern United States
A. a) Broad-tailed hummingbirds mi-

Broad-tailed hummingbirds

grate as far south as Mexico and Central America, returning each spring to feed on Rocky Mountain wild-flowers—that's a one-way trip of about 3,000 miles, all done by a bird no bigger than a cell phone.

Q. How big around are broad-tailed hummingbird nests?
a) Two inches   b) Three inches   c) Four inches
A. a) About two inches in diameter.

Beavers mate for life.

Q. How large is a broad-tailed hummingbird egg?
a) 0.5 x 0.35 inches   b) 1 x 2 inches   c) 1.25 x 2.50 inches
A. a) Their egg is about 0.5 x 0.35 inches, or only slightly larger than a grain of long-grain rice.

Q. How long do broad-tailed hummingbird chicks incubate?
a) Two weeks   b) Three weeks   c) Four weeks
A. a) Two weeks.

Q. How long does it take for a newly hatched broad-tailed hummingbird to attempt its first flight?
a) 14 days   b) 18 days   c) 32 days
A. b) About 18 days. The still-tiny bird leaves the nest for the last time around 21 days after hatching—talk about a short childhood.

Q. How can you identify a male rufous hummingbird?
a) They shine a red-gold color in the sunlight.
b) They have non-distinct coloration.
c) They incubate the eggs.
A. a) Under bright sunlight, they shine an intense red-gold color.

Q. Hummingbirds are a common sight and relatively well-studied animal in Rocky Mountain National Park. About how large are the bird bands used by researchers to track hummingbirds?
a) The size of a grape   b) The size of a fingernail
c) The size of a fishing hook's eye
A. c) About the size of the eye on a fishing hook. The band itself weighs roughly 6.6 milligrams, only about 0.2 percent the total weight of an average hummingbird—that's about the equivalent of an average size adult wearing a watch.

Q. Wearing bright clothing, especially red, can draw the attention of what animal?
a) Wild cattle   b) Mountain lions   c) Hummingbirds
A. c) Hummingbirds are attracted to bright-colored clothing. Mistaking vibrant colors for flowers, park hummingbirds may fly directly toward you. The same is true with the park's butterflies.

----

*The calliope hummingbird, a visitor here, is the
smallest hummingbird in the United States,
weighing about one tenth of an ounce.*

Q. What is the most common hummingbird in the park?
a) White-eared hummingbird   b) Ruby-throated hummingbird
c) Broad-tailed hummingbird
A. c) The broad-tailed hummingbird.

Q. There are more than 300 species of hummingbirds in the world. How many are found in Rocky Mountain National Park?
a) Three   b) Six   c) Eight
A. b) Six. They are: broad-tailed hummingbirds, rufous hummingbirds, black-chinned hummingbirds, calliope hummingbirds, ruby-throated hummingbirds, and magnificent hummingbirds.

Q. Place these hummingbirds in order of rarity in the park, from most to least seen: Rufous hummingbird, magnificent hummingbird, broad-tailed hummingbird, calliope hummingbird, ruby-throated hummingbird, black-chinned hummingbird.
A. From most to least seen, they are: broad-tailed hummingbird, rufous hummingbird, black-chinned hummingbird, calliope hummingbird, magnificent hummingbird, ruby-throated hummingbird.

Q. How many species of hummingbirds are found in Europe, Asia and Africa?
a) None   b) 50   c) 150
A. a) None. The hummingbird is a "New World" species, meaning they're found only in the Western Hemisphere.

Q. In 2004, scientists made a startling discover about hummingbirds. What was it?
a) Hummingbird fossils were found in an unlikely place.
b) Hummingbirds are related to pterodactyls.
c) Hummingbirds actively migrate across the Pacific Ocean.
A. a) Hummingbird fossils were found in an unlikely place: 30-million-year-old hummingbird fossils were found in Germany. Since there are no hummingbirds in Europe today, this confounded the scientific community. Common theory is that hummingbirds may have at one time been native to Europe, but have long since disappeared from the region. Today, hummingbirds are found only in the Western Hemisphere, which includes North, Central and South America.

An eagle nest is so well constructed that birds from later generations may use the same nests as their forebears.

Q. What colors are male broad-tailed hummingbirds?
a) Brown and gold   b) Green and red   c) Yellow and grey
A. b) Green and red.

Q. A broad-tailed hummingbird will make its nest out of lichens, moss and what?
a) Trash   b) Leaves   c) Spider webs
A. c) Spider webs. Deceptively strong for their size, the silken qualities of spider webs make ideal building material for the hummingbird's tiny nests.

Q. True or false: Both male and female broad-tailed hummingbirds participate in raising their chicks.
A. False. Only the female broad-tailed hummingbird raises the young.

Q. In spring, elk in the park have a noticeable animal riding on their backs. What is it?
a) Black-billed magpie   b) Abert's squirrel   c) Western tanager
A. a) Black-billed magpie.

Q. Why do black-billed magpies hitch a ride on the park's elk, especially in spring?
a) To save energy   b) To protect themselves from predators
c) To eat ticks
A. c) They are picking off and eating ticks. The elk, with no natural defense against the parasite, welcome the winged travelers.

Q. Do park magpies prefer to build their nests from scratch each spring, or just "refurbish" last year's construction?
A. While they will build new nests, magpies in the park prefer "fixer-uppers."

Q. Which owl found in Rocky Mountain National Park is the largest of the tufted owls in North America?
a) Barn owl   b) Great horned owl   c) Northern pygmy owl
A. c) The great horned owl, with a wingspan of up to five feet.

Did you know eagles migrate? In fact, they travel such great distances that eagles native to California have been spotted as far north as Alaska, and eagles often seen in Florida also roost in Michigan.

Q. During what month do the park's great horned owls search for mates?
a) January   b) February   c) March
A. a) January.

Q. True or false: The park's great horned owls migrate.
A. False. The great horned owl is a year-round resident of the park.

Q. In what month are baby great horned owls hatched?
a) March   b) April   c) May

A. a) March. A typical mating pair will have two eggs, though they may have as many as five at a time. Like other baby birds, each hatchling fights dearly for its parents' attention, often causing the weaker chicks to die.

Q. What is a "witch's broom" and what does it have to do with the park's great horned owls?
a) A type of tree growth
b) A bundle of dead wood
c) A ground squirrel's nest
A. a) A type of tree growth. Witch's brooms are areas of a tree where large numbers of limbs sprout from one area, creating what looks like the bristles of a broom. Great horned owls use these branches to build their nests.

Q. True or false: A great horned owl will only use a nest it constructs itself.
A. False. Great horned owls are opportunists, known to roost in previously occupied nests, especially those of fellow raptors.

Q. What night-time predator likes to hunt skunks?
a) Coyote   b) Owl   c) Fox
A. b) Owls, like the park's great horned varieties, are quick enough hunters that they can capture and dispatch a skunk before it releases its distinctive stink.

Christmas Bird Counts in Rocky Mountain National Park have recorded nearly 50 species of bird spending the winter here.

Q. Who sponsors the annual Christmas Bird Count in Rocky Mountain National Park, and around the globe?
a) The Junior Women's League   b) The National Audubon Society
c) The Rotary Club
A. The National Audubon Society sponsors the Christmas Bird Count. The count, which has been ongoing since 1900, takes place throughout North, Central and South America. To join the count, contact the National Audubon Society. Counters are made up of volunteers, and the society provides you with identification charts, so don't worry if you're not an experienced birder.

Fish
Q. How many fish species are found in Rocky Mountain National Park?
a) 3   b) 7   c) 11
A. c) 11. If you find yourself fishing in the park, you could reel in a western longnose sucker, western white sucker, mountain sucker, mottled sculpin, Colorado speckled dace, greenback cutthroat trout, Yellowstone cutthroat trout, Colorado River cutthroat trout, rainbow trout, eastern brook trout or a brown trout. Rocky Mountain National Park's species list is fairly lacking when compared to the rest of the region, where more than 100 fish species have been identified. The park's cold-water conditions is a main factor in the lack of more fish species.

Q. Of the 156 lakes in the park, how many contain self-sustaining fish populations?
a) 48   b) 124   c) All 156
A. a) 48. Only around 30 percent of the park's lakes contain self-supporting fish populations. The exceptionally high altitudes of some lakes prevent fish populations from spawning, due to cold temperatures.

Q. According to the National Park Service, how many species of trout are found swimming in Rocky Mountain National Park's waterways?
a) 2   b) 4   c) 6
A. c) Six: brown trout, brook trout, rainbow trout, Colorado

The use of lead sinkers or other fishing items made of lead is strongly discouraged in the park, for fish species' safety.

River cutthroat trout, Yellowstone cutthroat trout and greenback cutthroat trout.

Q. What are the only two native trout species in Rocky Mountain National Park?
a) Brook trout and greenback cutthroat
b) Brown trout and brook trout
c) Greenback cutthroat and Colorado River cutthroat
A. Greenback cutthroat and Colorado River cutthroat. All other trout, including rainbow, brook and brown trout, were introduced.

Q. When did the National Park Service stop stocking non-native fish in the national park?
a) 1947   b) 1969   c) 1981
A. b) The park stopped stocking non-native fish in 1969 in order to help increase the native populations. Non-native fish often out-compete local species, leading to a decline of the area's natural diversity. In fact, the Colorado state fish—the greenback cut-throat trout—was once thought to be gone from Colorado waters, largely in part to the introduction of other species. Luckily, these didn't completely disappear and are slowly making a comeback throughout the state.

Q. Who are the Greenback Backers?
a) The park's treasury council
b) Volunteers who help with fish conservation within the park
c) A group of backcountry backpackers
A. b) The Greenback Backers is a volunteer group (composed mostly of anglers) who assist park efforts in greenback cutthroat trout recovery. Among their volunteer duties are policing waters to ensure fellow anglers aren't catching and keeping this threat-ened fish, and assisting wildlife officials with egg collection and population counts.

The greenback cutthroat, Colorado's state fish, was once thought to be fished to extinction in Colorado. Luckily, a few fish were eventually found in a high-mountain stream and, with diligent stewardship, are making a robust comeback—though they are still federally listed as a threatened species.

Colorado River cutthroat trout live on the park's wetter west side, and greenback cutthroats on the drier east side.

Q. Brook trout and brown trout spawn during what season in the park?
a) Fall   b) Winter   c) Spring
A. a) Fall.

Q. Cutthroat and rainbow trout spawn during what season in the park?
a) Spring
b) Summer
c) Fall
A. Spring.

Cutthroat trout

Q. When not spawning, are male or female brook trout the more colorful sex?
A. Males are generally more colorful, but during spawning season, even the females develop a ruby color on their bellies.

Q. What are brook trout egg deposits called?
a) Redds   b) Roe   c) Hash
A. a) Redds. The female trout deposits her eggs on the river bottom, producing anywhere from 300 to 3,000 at a time. Once the eggs have been placed, male trout release milt and fertilizes the eggs. Trout are not known as doting parents; after the milt is released, the female trout roughly covers the eggs with river silt by flicking her tail then leaves the brood to hatch and fend for themselves.

---

*Wood frogs live only on Rocky Mountain National Park's west side—
and no one yet knows why.*

Amphibians, Reptiles & Insects

Q. What tiny animal warranted the invention of a special radio transmitter for scientific study in the park?
a) The wood frog   b) The tiger salamander
c) The broad-tailed hummingbird
A. a) The wood frog. A 0.6-gram transmitter was created and tested by Dr. Erin Muths in nearby Fort Collins, Colorado. Attached to the no-more-than-8-ounce frog by an elastic thread, these tiny transmitters relayed valuable location information to researches. It was discovered that wood frogs are not big on commuting. Wood frogs in the park barely traveled more than a few hundred yards from where they were hatched.

Q. How many amphibian species are found in Rocky Mountain National Park?
a) 5   b) 7   c) 12
A. a) 5: the tiger salamander, boreal toad, Western chorus frog, wood frog and Western terrestrial garter snake.

Q. What sound do tiger salamanders, one of the park's reptile species, make?
a) None   b) Grunts   c) Squeaks
A. a) None. Tiger salamanders lack the capability for vocalization.

Q. Where's the best place in Rocky Mountain National Park to increase your chances of seeing the hard-to-find tiger salamander?
a) Bear Lake   b) Lily Lake   c) Crystal Lake
A. b) Lily Lake, found in the park's southern reaches. Look to the lake's shallows for salamander sightings. These yellow and black banded amphibians are rare, and due to environmental factors their numbers are still decreasing.

Q. Boreal toads often hibernate in ground squirrel burrows and what other rodent's home?
a) Weasel dens   b) Skunk hollows   c) Beaver dams
A. c) Beaver dams.

Humans may call toads "ugly," but their skin surface is a great camouflage among the rocks of a riparian area.

Q. How much of their lives can boreal toads, a park resident, spend in hibernation?
a) One quarter of their lives
b) One third of their lives
c) Half of their lives
A. c) Up to half a boreal toad's life can be spent in hibernation.

Q. What is chytridiomycosis and what does it have to do with amphibians in Rocky Mountain National Park?
a) A disease that's threatening amphibian populations.
b) An invasive amphibian species from Asia.
c) There is no such thing as chytridiomycosis.
A. a) Chytridiomycosis is a disease among amphibians that has led to a great decline in populations numbers in the park, as well as world-wide.

Q. Amphibian populations are at risk globally, as well as in the park. What six factors are believed to be part of this decline?
A. Disease, climate change, chemical contamination, invasive species outcompeting local populations, over-harvesting, and habitat loss or habitat degradation.

Q. What cat-named frog is now extinct in the park, though it still lives in other areas of the world?
a) The lion toad   b) The tiger salamander   c) The leopard frog

A. c) The leopard frog. Due to habitat loss and predation prior to park conservation efforts, the leopard frog has been extirpated from Rocky Mountain National Park.

Q. True or false: Poisonous snakes are abundant in Rocky Mountain National Park.
A. False. There are no poisonous snakes in the park.

Park bumblebees prefer to make their homes in abandoned mouse holes. Researchers believe the bees are drawn to these holes because of the good insulation already added by the previous tenants.

Q. Queen bumblebees are often seen in the park during spring. On average, how large are these royal insects?
a) Between 0.5 and 0.75 inch   b) Between 0.75 and 1 inch
c) Between 1 and 1.25 inches
A. b) Queen bumblebees are between 0.75 and 1 inch in size. Drone bumblebees are much smaller, as is the more familiar and closely related honeybee.

Q. Butterflies and moths are abundant in Rocky Mountain National Park. How can you tell them apart?
a) By the food they eat   b) By the color of their wings
c) By their antennae
A. c) By their antennae. Moths have furry antennae, while butterflies have smooth antennae.

Q. What characteristic do butterflies and moths share with fish?
a) They have gills.   b) They both have scales.
c) They both see in infrared.
A. b) Much like a fish's defining feature, butterflies and moths have scales. Touching the delicate wings of either animal can scrape off these scales, damaging them and making it difficult for the animal to fly and ultimately survive. As with all wildlife, it's best to enjoy moths and butterflies without touching them.

The beautiful and delicate orange, black and white monarch butterfly is actually very poisonous to animals if eaten. In fact, their distinctive coloration acts as a warning to would-be predators. When reproducing, monarchs will only lay their eggs on milkweed which is itself a poisonous plant. This habitat choice aids in the insect's protection against predators such as grasshoppers. Unfortunately, some monarch populations, notably those found east of the Rocky Mountains, are in decline, probably due to reduced milkweed populations and other environmental factors.

Remove ticks promptly but carefully when they attach to your body, making sure to remove all the mouth parts, and not squeezing the tick bodies.

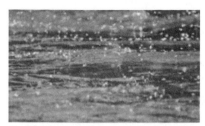

Caddisfly hatch rising off a stream.

Q. Caddisflies (a type of insect) are often seen near streams in the park. How many species of caddisflies are known to exist in North America?
a) 75   b) 550   c) 1,000
A. c) There are nearly 1,000 distinct species of caddisflies in North America.

Q. How many types of ticks are found in Rocky Mountain National Park?
a) 1   b) 2   c) 3
A. a) There is only one type of tick in Rocky Mountain National Park, the aptly named Rocky Mountain wood tick. While small, these parasites can pack a wallop, as a third of the population is thought to carry Colorado tick fever or the potentially deadly Rocky Mountain spotted fever.

Q. True or false: A tick is a type of insect.
A. False. Ticks, like the Rocky Mountain wood tick common in the national park, are actually arachnids. So what's the difference between an insect and an arachnid? One evident difference is that insects have six legs, while arachnids, like spiders and ticks, have eight. Ticks and other arachnids also lack the iconic antennae of an insect.

Q. How can you tell a female Rocky Mountain wood tick from a male?
a) Females are entirely brown in color.
b) Females have white markings on their back.
c) Males are brightly colored.
A. b) Female Rocky Mountain wood ticks are dark brown with a tint of red. They also display a white "shield" on their backs. Males are much less distinctive, with a tendency to be flatter and gray or reddish-brown in appearance.

Rocky Mountain spotted fever begins 3 to 14 days after exposure to an infected tick, with flu-like symptoms and perhaps red spots on the palms of the hands or the soles of the feet. See a doctor at once.

Q. Once engorged with blood, how large can a female Rocky Mountain wood tick get?
a) 0.25 inch   b) 0.5 inch   c) 1 inch

A. b) Well-fed female ticks are often measured at half an inch. It may still sound small, but consider the fact that they start out at around only $1/8$ an inch—that's an increase in body size of 37.5%! To put it in perspective, that weight gain would equate is a 100-pound person adding an extra 37.5 pounds after just one meal.

An enlarged view of female (left) and male Rocky Mountain wood ticks.

PLANTS

Pasqueflower

Q. Why is some snow in the park pinkish in color?
A. The pink snow gets its sunset hue from algae living among the ice crystals. While it may look like an inviting snow cone, treat it like its yellow-colored cousin. The algae blooming in the snow is actually toxic to humans and may have you running for the rest room due to its laxative effects.

Q. True or false: Wildflowers in Rocky Mountain National Park all bloom at generally the same time.
A. False. Wildflowers in the park bloom depending on their elevation.

Q. In what months do wildflowers begin to bloom in the park's lower elevations?
a) March and April   b) April and May   c) May and June
A. b) Flowers begin to bloom at lower elevation in late-April and early May.

Q. In what months do wildflowers begin to bloom in the park's higher elevations?
a) May and June   b) June and July   c) July and August

A. b) Sometime between June and mid-July wildflowers begin to light up higher elevations with colorful blooms.

Q. In which month do the aspens change from green to their distinctive gold?
a) August   b) September   c) October
A. b) Mid-September. While the middle of September is a general rule of thumb for fall color in Rocky Mountain National Park, there are myriad factors that can affect the date. A tree turning color depends greatly on weather conditions, including temperature, length of sun exposure and moisture content. For an added hitch in pegging a specific date, trees found at higher elevations turn color sooner than those rooted lower on the mountain.

Q. In Rocky Mountain National Park, there is a very obvious demarcation at a particular attitude where trees refuse to grow. What causes trees to stop growing at a certain altitude?
a) Sun exposure   b) Oxygen levels
c) Temperature
A. c) Temperature. Trees need an average temperature of about 50 degrees F to grow. The obvious treelines in the park are like giant almanacs of temperature patterns at altitude.

Q. What is the highest boundary of growing trees called?
a) The Green Line   b) Treeline
c) Flora Boundary
A. b) Treeline.

Longs Peak above treeline

Q. What two wildflowers in the park tend to be the earliest bloomers of spring?
a) Mountain candytuft, pasqueflowers
b) Avalanche lilies, yuccas   c) Louseworts, sego lilies
A. a) Mountain candytuft and pasqueflowers. These wildflowers often start blooming in mid-March.

"Alga" is the singular form of "algae."

Q. What blooming spring wildflower heralds the arrival of broad-tailed hummingbirds?
a) Glacier lilies   b) Wax currants   c) Globe flower
A. b) Wax currants *(Ribes cereum)*. These are the first flowers broad-tailed hummingbirds can feed on. Once other flowers begin to bloom, the hummingbirds will vary their selection.

> The waxflower, a native to the park, is a long-time inhabitant of Colorado. Fossils of the plant found in Colorado's Florissant Fossil Beds National Monument have been dated at 35 million years old.

Q. True or false: Albinism—the state of being albino—occurs in both plants and animals.
A. True. Though since they lack the life-sustaining chlorophyll—the substance that gives plants their green color—plants with albinism do not live long.

Q. What is "peat"?
a) A type of moss   b) A type of soil   c) A small mammal
A. b) Peat is a term for soil that's mainly made up of dead organic matter, such as rotting leaves or wood. Rocky Mountain National Park has a number of peat lands—or large areas composed of peat. Look for peat lands in waterlogged areas around seeps and abandoned beaver dams.

Q. Which of the following is not a type of peat land?
a) Bog   b) Glen   c) Fen
A. b) Glen. Fens, mires and bogs are all types of peat land. So, what's the difference? A fen is a peat land that is constantly wet from groundwater, as well as precipitation. A bog is a peat land that receives water only from precipitation. A mire is a peat land that's actively growing through a constant accumulation of organic matter.

Q. Engelmann spruce and ponderosa pine don't tend to grow above what altitude in the park?
a) 9,000-10,000 feet   b) 7,000-8,000 feet   c) 6,000-7,000 feet
A. a) 9,000-10,000 feet.

Rose hips (Rosa woodsii) *provide exceptionally high levels of Vitamin C. Rose hips are a favorite food of park bears and squirrels trying to fatten up prior to lean winters.*

Q. What is the boreal forest?
a) The northernmost ring of plant life around the globe.
b) A forest comprised only of short shrubs.
c) A forest that lacks animals.
A. a) The boreal forest is the name for the ring of plant life that encircles the globe at the northernmost point at which plants can grow. While well south of this ring, Rocky Mountain National Park's ecosystem still allows for the growth of plants normally only found in the boreal forest. Among these seemingly out-of-place plants is feather moss.

Q. From where does the name "boreal" forest come?
a) From Boreas, a Greek god.   b) From Boreala, a Norse god.
c) From Borealis, an Alaskan Native word.
A. a) Boreal comes from Boreas, the Greek god of the north wind. Since the boreal forest is known for being cold and windswept, the name is fitting.

Q. What are forbs?
a) Non-woody plants   b) A type of bird nest
c) A group of reptilian eggs
A. Forbs are non-woody plants, and are a popular food for the park's robust elk population.

Q. What's another name for five-needled pines?
a) Star pine   b) White pine   c) Pentacle pine
A. b) White pine. Limber pine is the only five-needled, white pine in Rocky Mountain National Park.

Q. Western figwort, also called bunny-in-the-grass, is a common, though unassuming, wildflower in Rocky Mountain National Park. Its "bunny-in-the-grass" moniker came from its resemblance to a rabbit's head, but how did it get its other name: "figwort"?
a) It was thought to cure hemorrhoids.
b) It tastes like a wild fig.   c) It was food for local frogs.

To protect viewing the night sky, both Rocky Mountain National Park and the town of Estes Park require shielded light fixtures in new or replacement buildings.

A. a) This particular wildflower was thought to hold medicinal qualities. "Fig" is an Old English word for hemorrhoids, while "wort" is applied to all medicinal plants. Whether this flower actually cures its Old English namesake is open for debate.

Q. How many species of figwort are found in Rocky Mountain National Park?
a) 33   b) 41   c) 59
A. b) 41.

Q. How many species of cacti are found in Rocky Mountain National Park?
a) Two   b) Five   c) Seven
A. a) Two: the plains prickly pear and the mountain ball cactus.

Q. How many flowering plants have been catalogued in Rocky Mountain National Park?
a) Fewer than 500   b) Between 950 and 1,000   c) More than 1,000
A. c) Rocky Mountain National Park is home to more than 1,000. In all, the state of Colorado claims approximately 3,200 flowering plant species.

Q. The park's alpine sunflower, also called the old-man-of-the-mountain, can take up to how many years to flower?
a) 30   b) 50   c) 70
A. c) 70. Some alpine sunflowers may take up to 70 years to bloom, though average bloom time is anywhere from 12 to 15 years. Once the alpine sunflower produces a flower, it dies. Because of this "one-and-done" approach to reproduction, this wildflower will wait until nutrients, light and ambient weather conditions are ideal before it blooms. The flower itself is bright yellow and ranges in height from just a few inches to nearly a foot tall.

Q. True or false: Scientists have documented every plant species in the park.
A. False. New plant species are constantly being discovered in Rocky Mountain National Park. Park officials are tight-lipped about providing specific information pertaining to new and rare species. According to the park, there are people who illegally collect and

---

The park's 37 species of mustard don't include any that can be used to make the popular condiment.

poach rare plants—keeping their identities and locations a secret help protect this resource.

Q. There is a variety of yellow composite wildflowers in the park, each nearly imperceptibly different from one another—even to the trained eyes of botanists. In fact, the frustration involved with identifying these flowers at a glance has earned them the acronym DYC. What does "DYC" stand for?
a) Darn Yellow Composites
b) Distinctive Yard Compost
c) Did You Check

Sunflowers

A. a) Darn Yellow Composites. Among members of the composite family—though not necessarily yellow—are daisies, asters, sunflowers, dandelions and goldenrods. These wildflower favorites are identified by their bunches of flowers that grow from a single base, looking like a bouquet displayed in a vase.

Q. What's a "composite" wildflower?
A. A composite indicates that the flowering portion of the plant is actually a mass of flowers, as opposed to a single bloom. Daisies and asters are part of the composite family.

Q. What makes a plant species "exotic"?
a) It is not common.   b) It comes from a tropical environment.
c) It is non-native.
A. c) A plant is said to be exotic if it is not native to the area. Rocky Mountain National Park is constantly under invasion from a variety of exotic species, including Canada thistle and toadflax.

Q. Why are non-native plants a concern to Rocky Mountain National Park?
A. Non-native species do not generally have natural predators, competitors, or even local diseases that can control their

---

When the park has removed non-native plants, the work was done without chemicals, through hand-pulling, cutting, chopping, scalding, and using insects to control the invaders.

populations. Since native species have to contend with each of these elements, non-native plants often out-compete the native varieties, ultimately leading to the disappearance of the native plants if left unmitigated.

Q. How many members of the iris family are found in Rocky Mountain National Park?
a) Three   b) Five   c) Seven
A. a) Three: the mountain iris, blue-eyed grass, and pallid blue-eyed grass.

Q. What function do the purple and yellow veins on a mountain iris' petals serve?
a) None that we are aware of>   b) They direct pollinators such as bees.   c) They are warnings about the plant's poisonous qualities.
A. b) They act like landing lights on a runway, directing bees and other pollinating insects to their nectar.

Q. The park's blue-eyed grass flowers open their petals only under what circumstances?
a) A certain amount of rainfall   b) A specific, constant temperature
c) Under direct, bright sunlight
A. c) Don't expect to see this wildflower on an overcast day, because they open their petals only under direct light (sunlight).

Q. The park's pallid blue eyed grass is exceptionally rare. The Colorado Natural Heritage Program lists them as having a G2 classification. What does that classification mean?
a) The species is in danger of disappearance throughout the world.
b) The species is found only in North America.
c) The species is in danger of disappearance in Colorado.
A. a) A G2 classification means the species is imperiled globally.

Q. What are GMOs?
a) Genetically Modified Organisms   b) Generally Mixed Organisms
c) Green Mossy Organisms
A. a) GMO stands for "Genetically Modified Organisms." A GMO is created, not through natural hybridization, but by physically taking a gene sequence from one plant or animal and inserting

---

Established in 1979, the Colorado Natural Heritage Program is a non-profit scientific organization affiliated with Colorado State University, which monitors the state's rare and endangered plants and animals.

it into another. In fact, this type of "gene jumping" can be done from plant to animal, such as when bacteria genes intertwine with plant sequencing.

Q. What effect do GMOs have on Rocky Mountain National Park?
a) They threaten to completely eradicate local species.
b) Scientists are unsure.   c) None whatsoever
A. b) Scientists are unsure of what effects GMOS will ultimately have on native plant species in the park.

Q. What park plant was once researched as a possible alternative rubber source during World War II, and was also used by Native Americans as a type of chewing gum?
a) Rocky Mountain rubber tree   b) Springbrush
c) Rubber rabbitbrush
A. c) Rubber rabbitbrush. American Indians made chewing gum from the plant's ground-up bark and stems, which contain little nutritional value. It was also used by native peoples as tea, cough syrup and a source for yellow dye. While it does contain the raw elements for rubber, extraction was too labor-intensive for the small product yield.

Q. What less-than-endearing name is the lichen *Diploschistes muscorum* better known as?
a) Carrion lichen   b) Cow pie lichen   c) Yellow-bellied lichen
A. b) Cow pie lichen. This oddly-named lichen owes its nickname to its appearance, which closely resembles a cow patty.

Q. Though you should refrain from eating it, what tasty-sounding name is the park's *Solorina crocea* lichen better known as?
a) Orange chocolate chip lichen   b) Vanilla fudge lichen
c) Banana strawberry lichen
A. a) Orange chocolate chip lichen. This lichen gets its vernacular name from its appearance. *Solorina crocea* is orange in color with brown elements embedded throughout, which look similar to chocolate chips.

Q. Though common in the park, lichen species are even better represented throughout the continent. How many lichen species

---

Rubber rabbitbrush provides a good winter forage for bighorn sheep, elk, and deer.

are known to exist throughout all of North America?
a) Less than 1,000   b) Between 3,000 and 3,500
c) More than 3,600
A. c) More than 3,600.

Q. What are apothecia?
a) A lichen's reproductive organs   b) A group of growing lichen
c) A rare lichen species
A. a) Apothecia are the reproductive organs of lichen and are composed of flat and cupped disks that carry spores.

Q. How many species of lilies grow in Rocky Mountain National Park?

Avalanche lily

a) 15   b) 20   c) 25
A. a) 15. Among them are wood lilies, which bloom beginning in July; mariposa or sego lilies with a bloom time from early July to mid-August; glacier or avalanche lilies, whose flowers are visible from mid-May to mid-August; alpine lilies that bloom from mid-June to late July; sand lilies, visible from early May to early June; and twisted-stalks, whose flowers display from mid-June to mid-August.

Q. What do onions, leeks and asparagus have in common?
a) They all evolved from a native Rocky Mountain National Park plant.
b) They all grow wild in Rocky Mountain National Park.
c) They are all types of lilies.
A. c) They are all members of the lily family.

Q. If you hear someone say they saw a "pink elephant" in the park, what are they talking about?
a) A type of wild animal   b) A flower
c) A former Rocky Mountain National Park mascot
A. a) A flower. Pink elephants, also called elephant heads, bloom from June to August, and as their name suggests, they look like pink pachyderms.

4,000 species of lily grow worldwide.

Q. How many species of lousewort (a type of vibrant wildflower that sends up spires of flowers) are found in Rocky Mountain National Park? How many are found in all of Colorado? The entire world?
a) Seven in Rocky Mountain National Park, nine in Colorado and 500 worldwide
b) Three in Rocky Mountain National Park, 10 in Colorado and 50 worldwide
c) One in Rocky Mountain National Park, four in Colorado and 100 worldwide
A. a) Seven species of lousewort grow in Rocky Mountain National Park, nine species grow in all of Colorado, and 500 are known worldwide.

Q. How did the wildflower species lousewort get its name?
A. Any plant with the word "wort" indicates it was once thought to hold medicinal qualities. Folklore says that livestock that ate this flower would contract lice (the plural of "louse"); modern science has found no actual evidence to support this.

Q. What are fairy rings?
a) Places where deer rest for the night   b) Swarms of gnats
c) Circles of mushrooms
A. c) Fairy rings are circles of growing mushrooms. Fairy rings are common in Rocky Mountain National Park, especially following a period of wet weather. These seemingly odd growths are actually the flowering bodies of a single fungus, found just beneath the soil.

If you see a grouping of growing mushrooms, they most likely are parts of the same organism and not individual plants.

Mushrooms and fungi are not the same thing. Mushrooms are actually the "flowers" of fungi, which live buried in decaying matter, most often out of sight.

Q. What are hyphae?
a) A rare type of park animal   b) Parts of fungi
c) The eggs of greenback cutthroat trout
A. b) Hyphae are slender white threads that connect the various parts of a fungus.

Q. In what ecological zone do you find the park's ponderosa pines?
a) Montane   b) Tundra   c) Alpine
A. a) Montane. The montane ecosystem extends from 5,500 feet to 9,000 feet in elevation and, is composed of ponderosa pines on warmer, south-facing slopes, while Douglas-fir forests grow on cooler, north-facing slopes.

Q. What does the bark of a mature ponderosa pine smell like?
a) Vanilla   b) Coffee   c) Cinnamon
A. a) Though not overpowering, the smell of ponderosa pine bark has a hint of vanilla.

Q. What's the best month to see wildflowers bloom in Rocky Mountain National Park?
a) May   b) June   c) July
A. c) July.

Q. How many species of grasses are found in the park?
a) 47   b) 73   c) 101
A. c) There are 101 types of grass in Rocky Mountain National Park, ranging from the spindly high-altitude Alpine Blue Grass to the wheat-like, lower-growing Prairie Junegrass.

Q. How many species of sedges are found in the park?
a) 34   b) 66   c) 97
A. b) 66.

Q. What is a sedge?
a) A specific type of plant   b) A specific type of animal
c) A favorite habitat of leopard frogs
A. a) A sedge is a plant variety with non-rounded stems, usually grass-like and found in riparian areas. The mnemonic device for remembering the definition of sedge is "Sedges have edges."

The montane ecosystem has soil that absorbs water and nurtures thicker, more lush ground cover than is seen at higher elevations.

Q. How many types of sedges are found in Rocky Mountain National Park?
a) 55   b) 65   c) 75
A. c) There are 75 sedge species that grow in Rocky Mountain National Park—a relatively small number compared to the 4,000 to 5,000 sedge species believed to be found worldwide.

Q. Why aren't sedge flowers generally very showy?
a) They don't need to attract pollinators.
b) They don't want to be eaten by deer and elk.
c) They lack pigmentation.
A. a) Sedges are wind pollinated, meaning they don't need to attract insects and other pollinators, which is usually the job of showy blooms.

Q. How far back do sedge species date in the fossil record?
a) Less than 33.6 million years
b) Between 54.8 and 33.7 million years
c) More than 55 million years
A. b) There is evidence in the fossil record of sedges in the Eocene, which took place 54.8 and 33.7 million years ago. This is the age when the first mammals were appearing on the planet.

Q. How many species of plants can be found in Rocky Mountain National Park?
a) 250   b) 500   c) 1,000
A. c) About 1,000. While this may seem like a staggering number, keep in mind, there are 300,000 recorded plant species spread throughout Colorado—and that isn't counting lichens.

Q. Most flowers in Rocky Mountain National Park fall into two categories: bilaterally symmetrical and radially symmetrical. What distinguishes one type from the other?
a) The way then can be divided   b) Their coloration
c) Their root systems
A. a) The way they can be divided. Bilaterally symmetrical flowers can be split down the center and one side will mirror the other—think of an orchid. Radially symmetrical means the flower

---

*Before a new-construction project, plant matter from the area
is collected for replanting on the disturbed land
after the project is completed.*

can be broken into infinitely equal parts—a daisy is a radially symmetrical flower.

Q. True or false: All plants in Rocky Mountain National Park use chlorophyll to create energy to survive.
A. False. Not all plants rely on photosynthesis for energy. In fact, some plants such as fungi survive on decaying matter, while others such as mistletoe are parasitic, stealing energy from other living plants.

Q. What is a saprophyte?
a) A plant that grows above 11,000 feet
b) A plant that can only survive when totally submerged in water
c) A plant that survives on decaying matter
A. c) A saprophyte is a plant that gets its energy not from the sun, but from decaying matter. The park's coral roots (members of the orchid family) are saprophytes.

Q. What are the four main parts of a flower?
a) Cup, pistil, stamen, petal   b) Pistil, stamen, sepal, petal
c) Pistil, stamen, nectar, petal
A. b) Pistil, stamen, sepal and petal.

Q. Do all flowers smell sweet?
A. No. Some flowers have no detectable smell, while others produce near tear-inducing stenches that seem closer to rotting meat than potpourri. The smells, while repulsive to us, are actually sweet scents to particular animals, including flies, which also serve as active pollinators.

Q. What is a diatom?
a) A type of snowflake   b) An algae classification
c) A germinating seed
A. b) A diatom is a classification of algae found in the park and throughout the world. This hardy plant has been known to grow more than 14 feet below the frozen waters of Antarctica.

Rocky Mountain National Park has its own greenhouse, where seeds gathered from native plants can be nurtured into healthy new plants.

Q. How many species of diatoms have been identified in Rocky Mountain National Park?
a) 31   b) 78   c) 138
A. b) 78. Because new diatom species are still being discovered in the scientific world, and because of a debate on what distinguishes one diatom species from another, the research world is split on the exact number of diatoms found worldwide; rough estimates range anywhere from 20,000 to 2 million diatom species.

Q. What do diatoms and window glass have in common?
a) They're both made of the same stuff.
b) They're both transparent   c) They both shatter easily
A. a) Window glass is made of silica, as are the cell walls of this tiny park plant. The sturdy cell-wall material prevents diatoms from decomposing, making it easier for scientists to study them going back thousands of years. Such research has created a better understanding of park environments before the incursion of man.

Q. What are catkins?
a) A type of environment   b) A type of furry park animal
c) A type of bloom
A. c) Catkins are a type of bloom, like those seen on pussy willows.

Q. What iconic Rocky Mountain tree blooms by producing catkins?
a) Aspen   b) Oak   c) Ponderosa pine
A. a) Aspen.

Q. What environmental factor is needed for aspen trees to bloom?
a) Constant temperature   b) Constant sunshine   c) Constant rain
A. a) Constant temperature. Temperatures must be above 54 degrees F for at least six consecutive days.

Q. How are aspen trees pollinated?
a) By bees   b) By birds   c) By the wind
A. c) By the wind.

Q. Why are aspen often referred to as "quaking" aspen?
A. The name "quaking aspen" comes from the constant flutter of an aspen's leaves. These leaves sport different shades of green

---

Two species of huckleberry help create ground cover in previously burned-over subalpine areas of the park.

on their tops and bottoms. The color difference exaggerates the fluttering motion. The stems of aspen leaves are also squared, not round like most other plants. This unique shape makes it easier for leaves to turn in a breeze than would a rounded form.

Q. Throughout Colorado, quaking aspens grow in a very specific elevation range. At what altitude do they grow?
a) Below 6,500 feet
b) Between 6,900 and 11,000 feet
c) Above 11,000 feet
A. b) Between 6,900 and 11,000 feet.

According to the National Forest Service, the aspen tree is the most widely distributed tree in North America, growing from northern Mexico, throughout the continental U.S., and up into Canada.

Q. What common evergreen in Rocky Mountain National Park was favored by the area's Ute Indians in building their easily moved homes?
a) Colorado blue spruce   b) Lodgepole pine   c) Douglas-fir
A. b) Lodgepole pine. Because of lodgepole's nearly ruler-straight trunks, these trees were ideal for constructing the movable houses used by Utes and other American Indian tribes.

Q. What's an ecomorph?
a) An animal that camouflages itself to look like area plants
b) A plant that can change its color
c) Two unrelated organisms that share characteristics
A. c) An ecomorph refers to two unrelated organisms that have evolved in much the same way. For example, Rocky Mountain National Park's yuccas and Hawaii's silverswords—found in Haleakala National Park—are examples of ecomorphs. These plants both

---

"Forest health" measures the diversity of trees and the habitats they provide for ground-cover plants and for animals, as well as the health of individual trees.

flower just once every six to twelve years before dying and send up a single tower of flowers. In addition to the way they flower, they also look alike in many ways, from their spike-like leaves to their vertical habit of growth.

Q. If you find yourself on a mountain standing between 8,000 and 9,500 feet in elevation within the park, and you are surrounded by Douglas-fir trees, on which side of the mountain are you most likely located?
a) North   b) South   c) East
A. a) North. Douglas-firs are more often found in the cooler and less-sunny north-facing side of slopes, while the south-facing slopes, with generally sunnier exposures, support junipers and ponderosa pines. These fir trees also prefer to grow between the very specific altitudes of 8,000 to 9,500 feet.

Q. What is a "krummholz" forest?
A. Krummholz forests are found along the ecological boundary of subalpine and alpine tundra. Due to harsh conditions at this dividing line, trees grow low to the ground, are often gnarled in appearance, and quixotically tend to live longer than their lower-elevation cousins.

Q. Found rooted at the higher reaches of the subalpine ecological area, subalpine fir, Engelmann spruce and limber pine are known as what type of trees?
a) Climax trees   b) Border trees   c) Highline trees
A. a) Climax trees.

Q. Overcrowding by what holiday-related plant helps lead to overpopulation of the voracious pine beetle?
a) Holly   b) Mistletoe   c) Douglas-fir
A. b) A parasitic plant, mistletoe saps the energy from trees, making them exponentially more susceptible to attack from the voracious pine beetle. Historically, the more mistletoe infestation there is in a forest, the less healthy the trees therein.

Q. What effect can an unchecked pine beetle population have on forests like those found in Rocky Mountain National Park?

In the alpine tundra ecosystem above treeline, plants that survive the extreme winds and cold winter temperatures are actually fragile— be careful where you step.

a) None   b) Near-complete devastation
c) Scientists are still unsure of their impact.
A. b) Near-complete devastation of trees and ultimately the forest as a whole.

Q. What environmental factor is often credited with the exponential increase in pine beetle-infected trees?
a) Unusually hot summers
b) Too much winter snowpack
c) Lack of traditionally cold winters
A. The lack of cold winters. Unusually higher winter temps over the past few years mean the drop in mercury that once led to a natural, and needed, die-off of pine beetles has not been occurring, allowing the mountain pine beetle to reproduce to the point of overpopulation. The pine beetle's destructive effects are evident, especially in the summer, when swaths of dead and dying trees are not green but turn brown and yellow as their needles die.

Q. Are mountain pine beetles native to the area, or have they been introduced?
A. They are native.

Q. How do pine trees in the park help protect themselves from mountain pine beetle attack?

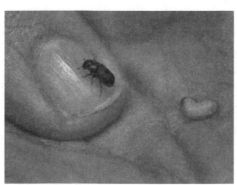

a) By attracting animals that feed on the beetles
b) By producing pitch
c) By growing thicker bark
A. They produce a substance called pitch. The pitch, sticky red or white excretions, serves to force the beetles out of their bored holes.

Adult pine bark beetle (on fingernail) and pupa (on palm)

Q. The pine beetle's relationship with park trees is far from symbiotic. While not welcomed by the host tree, the pine beetle does have a symbiotic

---

In the harsh alpine climate zone, a small flower might have a taproot extending three feet into the ground to reach water.

relationship with a specific organism. With what organism does the mountain pine beetle share this special relationship?
a) Ants   b) Fungus   c) Mistletoe
A. b) Fungus (*ceratocystis*). The mountain pine beetle is able to disperse the spores of this blue-stain fungus after it bores into the trunk of a tree. These spores colonize the hapless tree and effectively block pitch creation, allowing the mountain pine beetle an unhindered environment in which it can feed, grow and reproduce.

Q. Why do mountain pine beetles prefer larger trees in the park?
a) Larger trees provide more food and protection.
b) Smaller trees lack a certain needed nutrient.
c) Larger trees have a weaker defense.
A. c) Larger trees provide better food for the pine beetle and their thicker bark allows greater protection from predators and the climate.

Q. What are the life stages of a mountain pine beetle?
a) Pupa, adult
b) Egg, pupa, adult
c) Egg, larva, pupa, adult
A. c) Egg, larva, pupa, adult.

Q. What is "frass"?
a) Pupa pine beetles   b) A beetle's home   c) Beetle poop
A. c) Beetle poop. Technically, frass is partially digested wood particles, but you get the picture. Mountain pine beetles stuff frass into their egg galleries, where the next generation of this voracious beetle will gorge on the wood pulp until they're old enough to bore their own pathways into the tree or fly to a neighboring tree to restart the process.

Q. How can you tell if an otherwise healthy tree in the park is home to a mountain pine beetle?
A. Look for sawdust at the base of the tree. These mounds of sawdust are caused by the boring of a beetle.

Watch out for falling trees when camping, hiking, or driving through the park—especially on windy days or right after a snowstorm has covered the branches.

Q. Rocky Mountain National Park continually battles noxious plants. What exactly are "noxious plants"?
a) Poisonous plants   b) Non-native plants   c) Foul-smelling plants
A. b) Noxious plants are any non-native plant species that grows aggressively and has no natural controls in the area. Sweet clover and spotted knapweed are two of the park's most notorious noxious plants.

Q. As a caterpillar, the skipper butterfly will only eat muhly grass and nothing else. If muhly grass were ever to die off from the park, so too would the skipper butterfly. What is this symbiotic disappearance of species called?
a) Species disconnection
b) Mass disappearance
c) Co-extinction
A. c) Co-extinction.

Muhly grass

Q. True or false: Air pollutants lead to snow pollution as well as ice, lake, and soil pollution.
A. True. Pollution, especially nitrogen, released by fossil-fuel-burning factories and cars, is carried thousands of miles around the globe, often settling into water reserves. In fact, water, snowpack, and plants in the park are all showing increased levels of nitrogen.

Q. By what percent have nitrogen levels in the park been increasing since the 1980s?
a) 2%   b) 5%   c) 7%
A. a) By 2%, annually.

Q. Nitrogen is a common component in fertilizer, so why would that be bad for plant life in the park?
A. There is actually now more nitrogen in the soil than native

---

*When you arrive in the park, visit Beaver Meadows Visitor Center
to view the 23-minute movie about the park,* Spirit of the Mountains,
*and see aerial views of the high country and
close-ups of wildlife and wildflowers.*

plants can use, allowing excess nitrogen deposits to leech into water sources, causing acidification of lakes and streams.

Q. What is "blister rust"?
a) Rusting of a car's undercarriage   b) The wear done to trees by itchy bears   c) A type of tree fungus
A. a) Blister rust is a fungus that attacks the branches of white pines.

Q. What is the only tree in Rocky Mountain National Park in danger of contracting blister rust?
a) Ponderosa pine   b) Aspen   c) Limber pine
A. c) Limber pine. The fungus that causes blister rust only attacks white pine—and limber pine is the only white pine variety in the park.

Q. How do rangers cure trees infected with blister rust?
a) There is no cure.
b) A chemical spray
c) By hand-scraping off the infection
A. a) They don't. Once infected, a tree eventually dies.

Q. Pine trees in Rocky Mountain National Park, as well as pine trees elsewhere in the United States, have been infected by an introduced fungus, which causes blister rust. In an effort to eradicate this lethal fungus, forestry services declared war on the organism. Since there is no cure for blister rust, in order to combat the fungus, infected trees were chopped down. After four decades (1930-1971) the Forestry Service cried "uncle" upon realizing that their efforts were having little effect. How many trees were cut down during this failed siege?
a) 9.2 million   b) 11.5 million   c) 14.3 million

Lodgepole pine cones open up to release their seeds only after being heated by wildfire, and the seeds flourish in the fresh ashes and bare mineral soil to start new trees.

A. c) 14.3 million. Most plants were pulled or felled by hand, although 536,000 gallons of the chemical 2-4-5T was also employed, with most of it being released in Yellowstone National Park.

Q. During the National Park's war against the fungus that causes blister rust, they used the chemical 2-4-5T to destroy infected trees. By what other name is chemical 2-4-5T known?
a) Agent Orange   b) DDT   c) Mustard gas
A. Agent Orange—the same compound used in the war in Vietnam.

Ponderosa pine bark, as it ages, turns from gray-brown to cinnamon red.

HISTORY

Timeline of Rocky Mountain National Park

10,000 BCE: Clovis Paleo-Indian hunters enter the park as an ice age ends and glaciers begin to retreat.

6,000 BCE to 150 AD: Hunter-gatherers spend spring and summer months in what would later become Rocky Mountain National Park. Researchers believe these transient tribes may be the ancestors to many of today's American Indian tribes, including the Ute, Comanche, Goshiute and Shoshone.

1200 to 1300: Ute Indians settle at the sites of the modern-day towns of North Park and Middle Park, as well as in areas bordering Rocky Mountain National Park.

1500: Apache Indians establish themselves in the area.

1800: The first appearance of Arapaho Indians is noted.

1820: The Stephen A. Long Expedition are the first non-American Indians to see Longs Peak.

1843: Rufus B. Sage is first explorer to enter the east side of park and write about it.

1858: Joel Estes enters what is now Estes Park and starts a ranch.

1868: A group led by John Wesley Powell makes the first ascent of Longs Peak.

1871: Addie Alexander becomes the first woman to climb Longs Peak.

1873: MacGregor Ranch is established just north of Estes Park.

1874: Abner Sprague homesteads in Moraine Park, builds Sprague's Ranch (later Stead's Ranch) and establishes tourism and guest ranching in the park.

1876: The State of Colorado is created. Since Colorado is established 100 years after the signing of the Declaration of Independence, it is called "The Centennial State."

Abner Sprague

1895 to 1935: Grand Ditch is built to bring water from the western slope of the Rocky Mountains, over the Continental Divide and into the eastern plains. It is considered an engineering marvel and allows the arid plains to be cultivated for farming.

1905: The Stanley Hotel is built in Estes Park.

1907: Enos Mills starts to lobby Congress for the creation of Rocky Mountain National Park.

1915: September 4—Rocky Mountain National Park is created.

1916: The National Park Service is created.

1913 to 1920: Fall River Road is constructed, making it the first road to cross the Continental Divide. The road connects Estes Park and Grand Lake through Rocky Mountain National Park.

1929 to 1933: Trail Ridge Road is constructed and replaces Fall River Road as the main access route through the park.

1936: Hidden Valley becomes a ski area. It is purchased by the park and closed in 1992.

1939: Abner Sprague becomes the first paying park visitor at Rocky Mountain National Park. At the time, national parks charged automobile fees of from $1 to (at Yellowstone) $3.

1964: The Wilderness Act is passed by Congress, which later allows for further protection of the park.

1966: The National Historic Preservation Act passes and provides added protection for historic and prehistoric sites on federal lands, like those found in Rocky Mountain National Park.

1968: The Beaver Meadows Headquarters building is completed. It is declared a National Historic Landmark in 2002.

The first humans to live in the area of the future park were paleo-Indians who moved here 10,000 to 20,000 years ago.

1982: The Lawn Lake dam collapses. The subsequent flooding kills three people and swamps the town of Estes Park.

1992: The park is expanded by the purchase of the Lily Lake area.

2000: The new Fall River Visitor Center opens.

2004: Hidden Valley, once a ski area, is partially reopened for winter sledding.

2005: Park entrance fee becomes $20.

Q. Rocky Mountain National Park has a large collection of museum pieces representing the natural history of the area. How many catalogued natural-history objects does the park have in its possession?

a) 3,000   b) 8,500   c) 10,500

A. About 10,500. Within this collection are a variety of animal species, plant varieties and geological samples, among other items.

Q. How many catalogued animal skulls does Rocky Mountain National Park have in its collection?

a) 300   b) 400   c) 500

A. b) Nearly 400.

Q. How many butterfly species does Rocky Mountain National Park have catalogued in its museums?

a) 500   b) 1,000   c) 2,000

A. c) Almost 2,000.

Q. Rocky Mountain National Park manages an herbarium—a collection of dried plants representing a variety of species. Many of the plant samples were obtained by the Denver Botanic Gardens throughout the early 1930s. How many plants make up the park's extensive collection?

a) 2,000   b) 5,000   c) 7,000

A. b) Almost 5,000. The park's collection represents each of the area's ecological zones.

Estes Park was founded in 1859, and 50 years later the elegant Stanley Hotel opened and enhanced the town's resort offerings.

Q. How many culturally historic items do Rocky Mountain National Park museums have in their collection?
a) 23,000   b) 33,500   c) 40,500
A. b) Around 33,500 objects. This robust collection includes original furniture pieces from area homesteaders.

Q. How many catalogued archaeological items does Rocky Mountain National Park have in its possession?
a) 12,500   b) 18,900   c) 20,700

A. c) More than 20,700. These archaeological artifacts provide insight into the area's original occupants, especially the Ute and Arapaho Indian tribes.

Q. Paleo-Indians, the park's first human inhabitants, left behind objects made of stone, clay and what?
a) Copper   b) Bone   c) Gold
A. b) Bone. Many of the paleo-Indian tools found in the park were constructed of bone taken from area animals.

Q. How many prehistoric human sites have been found in Rocky Mountain National Park?
a) Less than 100   b) Between 200 and 250   c) More than 300
A.) More than 300. These historic sites range in altitude from 8,000 to 13,000 feet above sea level.

Q. Historically, which American Indian tribe is known to have been a well-established visitor to modern-day Rocky Mountain National Park?
a) The Arapahoe   b) The Navajo   c) The Ute
A. c) The Ute.

Q. True or false: American Indian tribes traditionally made their permanent homes in what is now Rocky Mountain National Park.
A. False. While the Ute Indians frequented the lower eleva-

In 1865, Jules Verne imagined an astronomical observatory atop Longs Peak for his sci-fi novel, From the Earth to the Moon.

tions of the park during warmer months, the relatively sparse

game and unpredict-able winter weather made this high-altitude region a destination better suited for warm-weather months only. The Utes were only transient guests during the warmer seasons.

Q. Ute Indian ceremonial vision quests were often held within what is now Rocky Mountain National Park. What specific area in the park was a common vision quest destination for the tribe?
a) The headwaters of the Colorado River
b) Hagues Peak   c) Old Man Mountain
A. c) Old Man Mountain.

Q. In what year was Rocky Mountain National Park created?
a) 1915   b) 1927   c) 1933
A. a) 1915, on September 4.

> Rocky Mountain National Park was created a year before there was an official government body to manage it. It became a park in 1915, while Congress didn't create the National Park Service until 1916.

Q. What quintessential event led to the acquisition of land that would later become Rocky Mountain National Park?
a) The Louisiana Purchase   b) Lewis and Clark's expedition
c) Zebulon Pike's survey
A. a) The Louisiana Purchase. If high school history classes taught us anything, it was that Napoleon gave the fledgling United States the deal of the century when he sold 828,000 square miles of untouched New World wilderness to the government for $15 million—that's less than five cents an acre. Within that vast swath of land once claimed by Spain and

---

Elkanah Lamb and his son Carlyle were the first Longs Peak guides in 1875, charging $5 per trip.

then France was today's Rocky Mountain National Park.

Q. What English nobleman once owned roughly 8,000 acres of land in and around today's national park?
a) The Fourth Earl of Dunraven and Mountearl
b) The Second Duke of Manchester   c) The Sixth Earl of Wales
A. a) Windham Thomas Wyndham-Quinn, the fourth Earl of Dunraven and Mountearl, and Undersecretary for the Colonies. He began acquiring land—including the spot on which the Stanley Hotel currently sits—from 1873 to 1874. Eventually, after bowing to pressure to sell from local homesteaders who disliked the Earl's geographical monopoly, he sold off his land in 1907; 6,000 acres of which went to B.D. Sanborn of Greeley, Colorado and F.O. Stanley, inventor of the Stanley Steamer automobile.

Q. Hallett Peak, a 12,713-foot peak rising from the Continental Divide within the park, draws its name from one of the area's first residents. Besides his namesake peak, for what is Mr. Hallett best known?
a) He was the first mayor of Golden, Colorado.
b) He was the first Westerner to officially survey the area.
c) He started the state's first-ever climbing club.
A. c) An avid outdoorsman, William L. Hallett shared his passion

for conquering peaks with other climbers by founding the state's first climbing club.

Q. In what year was Colorado's first climbing club founded?
a) 1898   b) 1913   c) 1922
A. a) 1898. William L. Hallett, a local rancher in the Rocky Mountain National Park-area founded his climbing club at the turn of the century. In homage to Mr. Hallett's contributions to high-altitude pursuits, the 12,713-foot Hallett Peak—located within Rocky Mountain National Park—was named in his honor.

You can still visit Enos Mills' cabin. Built in 1885 at the base of Twin Sisters Mountain, it now operates as a museum and nature center.

Q. How large was the area first proposed for Rocky Mountain National Park?
a) 100 square miles   b) 500 square miles   c) 1,000 square miles
A. 1,000 square miles. Today it stands at 823 acres.

Q. Before the expansion to its current size, how many square miles did the park originally cover?
a) 358.5 square miles   b) 420.3 square miles
c) 541.9 square miles
A. a) 358.5 square miles, that's about 50 square miles larger than New York City.

Q. In what year did Congress approve the addition of 465 more acres to Rocky Mountain National Park?

Joel and Patsy Estes

a) 1897   b) 1956   c) 1990
A. c) 1990. In 1990, the U.S. Congress voted to expand Rocky Mountain National Parks' size with the addition of 465 more acres—that's three times the size of Washington DC's National Mall.

Q. Who was the first Westerner credited with settling in the area now known as Rocky Mountain National Park?
a) Horace Greeley
b) Zebulon Pike
c) Joel Estes
A. a) Joel Estes. Never heard of him? Well, he's a big name in the Rocky Mountain National Park region. In fact, the park's eastern border abuts the town of Estes Park, a vacation-centered town named for the area's first settler. Unfortunately for Joel, the winters were unfavorably harsh—as local Ute Indians had long known—and he later relocated to warmer Colorado environs.

In the 1890s, the regional mining boom began to fade away.

Q. In what year did the area's first settler, Joel Estes, build a permanent settlement in modern-day Rocky Mountain National Park?
a) 1860   b) 1890   c) 1912
A. b) 1860.

Q. From which U.S. state did Joel Estes emigrate before settling in Rocky Mountain National Park?
a) New York   b) Kentucky   c) Ohio
A. b) Kentucky.

Q. In what year did Rufus Sage publish *Scenes in the Rocky Mountains*, considered by many to be the first literary piece dedicated to the Rocky Mountain National Park-area?
a) 1910   b) 1843   c) 1899
A. b) While arguably filled with exaggerated information, Rufus provided his own report of the Rocky Mountains in 1843.

Q. What famed explorer—more often associated with the Grand Canyon—once climbed Rocky Mountain National Park's Longs Peak?
a) Meriwether Lewis   b) Zebulon Pike   c) John Wesley Powell
A. John Wesley Powell. Though better known for his exploration of the Grand Canyon and its surrounding lands, John Wesley Powell climbed the 14,259-foot Longs Peak in 1868.

Q. What American entrepreneur built the now-historic Stanley Hotel, located in neighboring Estes Park?
a) John Stanley   b) Percival Stanley   c) F.O. Stanley
A. c) F.O. Stanley. F.O. Stanley's name may seem unfamiliar until you pair it with his patented invention, the Stanley Steamer—a steam-driven car.

1903 Stanley Steamer runabout

Q. In what year did F.O. Stanley first visit Rocky Mountain National Park, arguably setting the stage for his investment in the park's neighboring town of Estes Park?

The ballad "Rocky Mountain High" by John Denver is one of Colorado's official songs.

a) 1903 b) 1923 c) 1947
A. a) 1903.

Q. Why did F.O. Stanley originally decide to visit the Rocky Mountain National Park region?
a) To hunt elk b) To escape taxes c) To improve his health
A. c) To improve his health. Owing his trip to the advice of his doctors, he traveled from Maine to Rocky Mountains for its dry air.

Q. F.O. Stanley is largely credited with helping inspire and organize the area's first consolidated conservation effort. What was the name of this altruistic organization?
a) Colorado Mountain Climbers Association
b) United Trail Workers of the Rocky Mountain Region
c) Estes Park Protective and Improvement Association
A. Estes Park Protective and Improvement Association.

Q. Who first proposed the idea of creating Rocky Mountain National Park?
a) President Roosevelt b) Enos Mills c) F.O. Stanley
A. Enos Mills.

Q. Who was Enos Mills?
A. Called the "Father of Rocky Mountain National Park," Enos A. Mills was born in Kansas in 1870 and moved to Colorado in his teen years. When he was 15 he made his first ascent of the 14,259-foot Longs Peak. Throughout his life, he made the trip roughly 40 times by himself and nearly 300 additional times as a guide. Before his death in 1922, Enos advocated for the creation of Rocky Mountain National Park—a feat which was eventually accomplished in 1915, seven years before his death.

Rocky Mountain National Park was the 10th national park created in the United States.

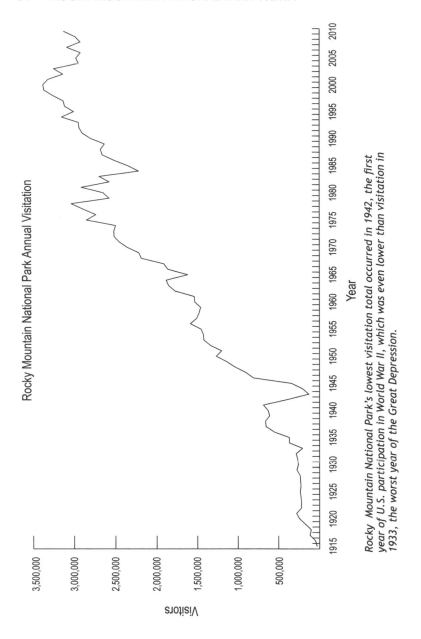

Rocky Mountain National Park Annual Visitation

Visitors

Year

Rocky Mountain National Park's lowest visitation total occurred in 1942, the first year of U.S. participation in World War II, which was even lower than visitation in 1933, the worst year of the Great Depression.

Park Superintendent Claude Way, in 1917, conspired with a young lady who announced she'd be touring the park with no clothes, weapons, or companions. It was a stunt to publicize the new national park, and the "Estes Eve" actually stayed in a lodge.

Q. True or false: An 18-hole golf course was once located within the park's modern-day boundaries.
A. False. It was a nine-hole golf course. Moraine Park was a forest-surrounded course. The course was eventually removed by the park system with the intent of returning the land to its natural state.

Q. True or false: Rocky Mountain National Park once housed an alpine ski area.
A. True. Hidden Valley opened in 1955 and featured 1,200 skiable acres. After being purchased by the park system, the area was eventually closed in 1991 and the land was allowed to be reclaimed by nature, though sledding is still a popular activity in the area.

Q. In what year was the park's backcountry permitting initiated?
a) 1964   b) 1972   c) 1987
A. b) 1972. The backcountry permitting process allows backpackers and campers access into hidden park areas, accessible only by hiking. While hikers are allowed entry into backcountry areas without a permit, those wishing to stay the night in those areas must first receive a backcountry permit.

Q. What designation has the United Nations bestowed upon Rocky Mountain National Park?
A. The United Nations' Man Biosphere program has designated Rocky Mountain National Park a Biosphere Reserve. The park was given this designation in recognition of its devotion to conservation of nature and genetic material, as well as its value as a site for cultural research.

Q. In what year did Rocky Mountain National Park license its first female nature guides?
a) 1917   b) 1942   c) 1963
A. a) 1917.

Q. What was so special about Rocky Mountain National Park's licensing of woman nature guides?

Moraine Park, now part of Rocky Mountain National Park, once was a booming resort town with multiple lodges and other facilities for tourist.

a) They were the nation's first female guides.
b) They were identical twin sisters.
c) They were related to President Teddy Roosevelt.
A. They were the nation's first female nature guides. Sisters Ester and Elizabeth Burnell held that honor in 1917. Both were expert guides who learned their craft from park proponent Enos Mills.

Q. What two hiking trails in Rocky Mountain National Park are themselves registered by the Federal Government as Historic Properties?
a) East Inlet, Fern-Odesa   b) North Inlet, Wild Basin
c) Bear Lake, Adams Falls
A. a) East Inlet and Fern-Odesa Trail. Both trails connect important historical and natural aspects of the park, including lodges, waterfalls and lakes, among other sites.

Q. The McGraw Ranch, located in Rocky Mountain National Park, was once a dude ranch. What function does it serve today?
a) Power station   b) Storage facility   c) Research center
A. c) A working research center. Today, McGraw Ranch is used by the Continental Divide Research Learning Center to research better ways to steward the natural and historical features of Rocky Mountain National Park.

Q. The McGraw Ranch is a type of historic site defined as a "vernacular landscape." What does that mean?
a) A property in danger of collapsing
b) A property whose purpose has changed over time

In 1932, an adventurous individual named Clerin "Zumie" Zumwalt climbed Longs Peak 53 times.

c) A landscape molded by both animals and humans
A. b) A vernacular landscape refers to a piece of property or structure whose purpose has changed over its lifetime. This makes it an interesting challenge for historic preservationists determined to accurately refurbish these locations—which iteration of the site should it represent? In the case of McGraw Ranch, historians wrestled with the question of restoring it as a dude ranch, a working cattle ranch or something else. After much thought, historians rebuilt it as it would have appeared between 1935 and 1955, when it served as a dude ranch.

Q. In what year were commercial air charter tours banned from the park's air space?
a) 1963   b) 1972   c) 1998
A. c) 1998. The ban was enacted to ensure park visitors would enjoy the sounds of nature, uninhibited by the thunderous noises of circling aircraft.

Q. How many other national parks in the western United States have bans on air travel?
a) None   b) One   c) Three
A. a) None. Rocky Mountain National Park is the only western park to enact and enforce a ban on air traffic.

Q. What is the most-visited historic site in the park?
a) Timber Creek Campground   b) Willow Park

c) The Holzwarth Never Summer Ranch
A. c) The Holzwarth Never Summer Ranch.

Q. Along what river are the historic Holzwarth cabins located?
a) The Gunnison River   b) The Platte River   c) The Colorado River
A. c) The Colorado River. Now a historical stop that provides a look into life in a 1920's dude ranch, the Holzwarth Cabins were originally offered to ranch guests at $2 a night.

Holzwarth Never Summer Ranch site includes a dozen cabins from this old-time guest ranch.

Q. Who was the first guest to enter Rocky Mountain National Park?
a) Abner Sprague   b) Josephine Spinner   c) Jeremy Long

A. a) In 1939, Abner Sprague, the local homesteader and lodge keeper, was the first paying customer to enter Rocky Mountain National Park. His cost for entry was less than $3—that high fee was charged then only for an auto entering Yellowstone National Park. Today, entrance fees are $20 for each car entering the park and $10 for bicycles, motorcycles and pedestrians.

In 2007, Rocky Mountain National Park became a model for the "climate-friendly park" ideal within the national park system. Goals set at the time included expanding visitors' shuttle bus usage and changing park vehicles to the best technology for decreasing greenhouse gas emissions. Other portions of the plan covered light bulbs and solar panels,

environment monitoring, and educating park visitors about what they can do here and at home to help the planet.

RECREATION

Q. How old was the oldest individual to climb to the summit of Longs Peak?
a) 85   b) 89   c) 93
A. a) 85. Reverend William Butler climbed to the pinnacle of Longs Peak on September 2, 1926, his 85th birthday.

Q. What nearby town was named for the area's first settler
a) Nederland, Colorado   b) Greeley, Colorado
c) Estes Park, Colorado
A. Estes Park, now the main entryway into Rocky Mountain National Park, was once a small community that quickly grew to support the needs of area visitors. Today, most of the area's accommodations, restaurants and park-based excursions are found in this mountain town.

Q. On average, how many visitors spend time in Estes Park, the town found along Rocky Mountain National Park's eastern portal?
a) More than 2 million   b) About 2 million   c) About 1 million
A. a) More than 2 million visitors find themselves in Estes Park annually. Many take advantage of the town's accommodations, visiting the park on a day trip. This method of stay is extremely

popular during the park's peak summer visiting months, when the park's 586 established camp sites and 267 backcountry tent areas fill quickly.

Q. How many visitors did Rocky Mountain National Park host in 2010?
a) 1,994,874   b) 2,687,251   c) 3,128,446
A. c) 3,128,446—that's equivalent to the entire population of Idaho visiting the park 2.5 times in 2010.

Q. In 2010, what month saw the most visitations?
a) June   b) July   c) August
A. b) July. With 699,101 visitors, July was head and shoulders above any other month that year.

Q. In what month in 2010 was the park visited the least?
a) December   b) January   c) February
A. c) With just 51,411 people entering the park, the month of February, 2010, saw the least amount of visitation.

Q. How many park rangers are on duty in a typical summer?
a) 47   b) 92   c) 103
A. b) The park employs 92 rangers during the summer. That means that during July of 2010, the park's busiest month that year, there was one park ranger for every 7,599 visitors.

Q. How many park rangers does the park employ in the winter?
a) 36   b) 43   c) 57
A. a) There are 36 park rangers employed by Rocky Mountain National Park in the winter. In February of 2010, the park's slowest visitation month of the year, there was one ranger for every 1,428 visitors.

Through Rocky Mountain National Park resources, visitors can locate private guides for bicycling touring, fishing, and technical climbing.

Q. How many backcountry permits were issued in 2010?
a) Less than 3,000   b) More than 3,000 but less than 6,000
c) More than 6,000
A. c) More than 6,000. The park issued 6,498 permits in 2010, which incorporated 33,392 user nights. It would take one camper roughly 91.5 years worth of overnight camping to manage that number alone.

Q. How many people camped in the park's three main camping areas—Glacier Basin, Moraine Park and Aspenglen—in 2011?
a) Less than 30,000   b) More than 30,000 but less than 50,000
c) More than 60,000
A. c) 66,343 visitors spent the night in the park's three main camping areas in 2011. That's more than 2.5 times the undergraduate student body of the University of Colorado.

Q. How much does a backcountry permit cost?
a) Nothing, it's free.   b) $5   c) $10
A. a) A backcountry permit is absolutely free. The park service uses the permits to monitor site usage and keep areas from being "loved to death."

Q. How many recreational all-terrain vehicles are permitted within the park at any time?
a) No ATVs are allowed within the park.   b) No more than 50.
c) There is no limit.
A. a) All-terrain vehicles are strictly forbidden within the park. ATVs are considered too detrimental to the fragile ecosystems found within Rocky Mountain National Park. In addition, the relatively loud noise of these vehicles distracts other visitors from the park's natural sounds and frightens away already bashful wildlife.

Q. Where is the only location within the park where snowmobiling is allowed?
a) Nowhere in the park is snowmobiling allowed.
b) Along Trail Ridge Road
c) A route that connects nearby Arapaho National Forest to the town of Grand Lake
A. c) The only snowmobiling allowed within Rocky Mountain Na-

---

Several approved concessionaires offer horseback riding in the park.

tional Park is a short easement connecting Arapaho National Forest to the town of Grand Lake. Much like ATVs/OHVs, snowmobiles are considered too detrimental to the park's natural assets to be allowed a significant place on park trails. And, as with all-terrain vehicles, the noise produced from a snow machine detracts from the experience of other park visitors.

Q. True or false: Bicycling within the park is allowed on both paved roads and unpaved trails.
A. False. Bike riding in the park is reserved solely for on-road cycling. All bicycles are barred from the park's trail system.

Q. Name the three main cycling routes found in Rocky Mountain National Park.
a) Trail Ridge Road, Old Forge Road, Eagle Pass
b) Horseshoe Park/Estes Park Loop, Eagle Pass, Summit Highway
c) Trail Ridge Road, Bear Lake Road, Horseshoe Park/Estes Park Loop
A. c) Trail Ridge Road, Bear Lake Road and Horseshoe Park/Estes Park Loop.

Q. In which Rocky Mountain National Park lake is fishing not allowed?

a) Bear Lake   b) Eagle Lake   c) Elk Lake
A. a) Bear Lake. While catch-and-release fishing is allowed throughout the park, anglers are forbidden from dropping a line into Bear Lake. Other areas closed to fishing include Bench Lake, Ptarmigan Creek, Hunters Creek, Lake Nanita Outlet and parts of South Fork Poudre River, Upper Columbine Creek and Lily Lake. Native greenback cutthroat trout, a federal and state Threatened Species, were restored in Bear Lake. Because the area is so heavily visited, it was decided that this would be an area where visitors can observe this threatened fish rather than catching it.

Trailbikes, mopeds, and bicycles are prohibited off the established roads in Rocky Mountain National Park. Nearby, Arapaho and Roosevelt national forests offer off-road trails for backcountry cycling.

Q. True or false: Horseback riding is not allowed in Rocky Mountain National Park.
A. False.

Q. What is special about the feed required for all domesticated livestock—like trail horses—entering Rocky Mountain National Park?
a) All feed must be certified weed-free.
b) All feed must be certified organic by the USDA.
c) No grain-based feeds are allowed.
A. a) All feed must be certified weed-free. To mitigate the presence of non-native and invasive plants within the park, all livestock entering the park are allowed only a diet of certified weed-free feed to prevent unwanted seeds from hitching a ride in hay bales. Non-native plants are a problem for many national parks and forests. These foreign invaders often out-compete the local flora, eventually squeezing them out of their areas and forever changing the landscape of important natural areas.

Q. How long is the hiking trail to the summit of 14,259-foot Longs Peak?
a) 4.4 miles   b) 7.5 miles   c) 10.3 miles
A. b) 7.5 miles, one way. While to some this may seem like a manageable day hike, consider that in those 7.5 miles, the trail gains 4,850 feet, just 430 feet shy of a mile skyward, all at a lung-burning altitude of 2.7 miles about sea level.

Q. True or false: Conditions along the trail to the top of Longs Peak are always free of inclement weather in the *summer* months.
A. False. Not only are electrical storms an ordinary occurrence, but snow, sleet and hail are common summer weather patterns atop Longs Peak.

Q. To complete a successful climb up Longs Peak, at what time does the park service advise you to start?
a) 3 a.m.   b) 5 a.m.   c) 7 a.m.
A. a) 3 a.m. If you plan on climbing the park's highest points, and one of the highest in the Continental United States, you better be prepared for an early start.

Ranger-led, two-hour snowshoe tours teach snowshoe basics, winter outdoor safety, and subalpine ecology; reservations required.

Q. At what time does the park service suggest you begin your descent from the summit of Longs Peak?
a) Noon   b) 1 p.m.   c) 3 p.m.

A. a) Noon. Afternoons often bring weather systems that can be dangerous to hikers caught on the trail. A smart hiker will complete the trip before the all-too-common afternoon storms strike.

Q. About how much time does the park system advise hikers to budget for a round-trip to the summit of Longs Peak and back?
a) 4 to 5 hours   b) 6 to 10 hours   c) 8 to 15 hours
A. c) Because of variable weather conditions and hiker ability, the park system advises scheduling anywhere between 8 and 15 hours to complete this strenuous hike.

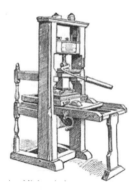

Q. What is the name of Rocky Mountain National Park's visitor newsletter?
a) *Rocky Mountain Times*   b) *High Country Headlines*
c) *The Rocky Reader*
A. b) *High Country Headlines*. The park's free visitor newsletter is constantly filled with updated information on park happenings and useful facts. Be sure to pick up a copy, at any visitor station, to supplement your travel guide.

Q. How many hours of volunteer service did the Nerd Herd—a group of tech-savvy volunteers—provide the park in 2009?
a) 3,200 hours   b) 3,900 hours   c) 4,500 hours
A. c) 4,500 hours.

Q. On average, how many annual man-hours do volunteers provide to Rocky Mountain National Park?
a) 50,000   b) 100,000   c) 150,000
A. b) 100,000, which works out to about 48 full-time employees.

Hikers who desire or need to walk or wheel on level trails can choose from the Coyote Valley, Sprague Lake, Lily Lake, and Bear Lake trails.

Rocky Mountain National Park is always looking for volunteers. To offer your time and services to the park, call 970-586-1330 or visit www.nps.gov/romo. Just remember, volunteering at Rocky Mountain National Park isn't for everyone—with high elevations and constantly changing weather patterns, a certain level of physical activity is required for many volunteer positions.

Q. How many e-mail queries from visitors did the park receive in 2007?
a) 5,893   b) 6,087   c) 7,052
A. b) 6,087, most of which are answered by a well-trained volunteer staff.

Q. How many phone calls did the park's Information Office receive in 2007?
a) Fewer Than 20,000   b) Between 20,000 and 25,000
c) More than 40,000
A. c) More than 40,000. That's about 110 calls every day. And like e-mail responses, the vast majority of these calls are handled by a veritable army of dedicated volunteers.

Q. On what days is Rocky Mountain National Park closed?
a) Christmas   b) New Year's   c) None, Rocky Mountain National Park never closes.
A. c) None. Rocky Mountain National Park is open year-round. Wildfires sometimes close portions of the park, the fall elk rut always closes portions, but the park never entirely shuts to visitors. The visitor centers, however, do follow a schedule. If you want to spend some time at one of the park's visitor centers, be sure to check in advance for its hours of operation.

Q. Weddings are popular in Rocky Mountain National Park. In fact, so much so that the National Park System has put a price on getting married in the park. How much should a couple expect to spend to be given the privilege of being married within the park?
a) $100   b) $150   c) $200

Sprague Lake Accessible Backcountry Campsite offers accessible picnic tables and vault toilet, and accessible parking space a half mile away on a level trail.

A. b) $150, but normal entrance fees are still required for each vehicle entering the park. Because of the delicate nature of the park, wedding groups need to be limited in number. If you want to get married in the park, you'll need to keep your attendance to no more than 100—including the photographer and officiant.

ENGINEERING &
CONSTRUCTION

Beaver Meadows Visitor Center

Q. Tom Casey, the architect of the Beaver Meadows Visitor Center, was a student of which great American architect?
a) George B. Post
b) Frank Gehry
c) Frank Lloyd Wright
A. c) Frank Lloyd Wright.

Q. True or false: Trail Ridge Road was the first road leading through the park.
A. False. The first road was Fall River Road, constructed in 1921.

Q. How was the route for Fall River Road chosen?
a) It followed the natural features of the mountain.
b) It followed an old American Indian hunting trail.
c) It followed an already-established county boundary.
A. b) Fall River Road follows a once well-worn path made by American Indian hunters.

Q. What type of vehicle is not allowed to travel on Fall River Road?
a) Any gas-powered vehicle
b) Any vehicle that has not passed an air-quality test
c) Any vehicle longer than 25 feet
A. c) Any vehicle longer than 25 feet. For safety reasons, any vehicle hauling a trailer or RV should not attempt Fall River Road. This narrow switchback-laden gravel road was not built with today's mobile-home traveler in mind.

Q. A popular stop along Fall River Road is Chasm Falls. How tall is these majestic waterfall?
a) 20 feet   b) 30 feet   c) 40 feet
A. b) It is about 30 feet high.

Q. How long is Fall River Road, the first roadway built into Rocky Mountain National Park?
a) 11 miles   b) 13 miles   c) 17 miles
A. a) 11 miles.

Q. What's the top speed limit along narrow Fall River Road?
a) 15 miles an hour   b) 25 miles an hour   c) 35 miles an hour
A. a) 15 miles an hour. When driving Fall River Road, even the snail-paced speed of 15 miles an hour may still seem too fast to a jittery driver.

Q. What is the highest point along Fall River Road?
a) 10,492 feet   b) 11,796 feet   c) 12,251 feet
A. b) 11,796 feet

Q. Oddly, a well-constructed outhouse in the park that stands on the site of the McGraw Ranch was later repurposed for what?
a) A phone booth   b) An office   c) A utility room
A. a) A phone booth. In fact, this privy-turned-Superman's-closet is now referred to as "The Phone Booth." While not much is known about the commode, this circa 1884 two-hole outhouse was intricately constructed in the Victorian Stick style—the same style of construction used to build the Mark Twain House and Museum in Connecticut.

The three-mile stretch that connects Fall River Road to Chasm Falls was built exclusively by convicts, who worked with nothing more than hand tools.

Q. What architectural philosophy was utilized in designing and constructing the Beaver Meadows Visitor Center?
a) Expressionist Modern Architecture   b) Organic Architecture
c) Art Deco
A. b) Organic Architecture. This style of design, championed by Frank Lloyd Wright and his protégés (who designed the visitor center), sought to create buildings that would exist in harmony with their surrounding landscapes.

Q. What growing organisms were important in the selection of sandstone used to build Beaver Meadows Visitor Center's exterior walls?
a) Ivy   b) Moss
c) Lichen
A. c) Lichen. When constructing Beaver

Rhizoplaca chrysoleuca *lichen growing on rock*

Meadows, the use of native and natural resources was tantamount. Part of the natural weathering integral to local sandstone is the growth of lichen on its surface. When selecting stone, masons were sure to choose pieces with robust lichen populations already intact.

Q. True or false: Lichen are actually composed of two distinct organisms.
A. True. Lichen, which we generally refer to as one organism, are actually two distinct creatures. A symbiotic relationship between algae and fungus create what we know as lichen. How does this partnership work? The chlorophyll-containing algae turns sunlight into food for the two organisms, while the fungus creates a hardened lattice to which the algae can cling and grow.

Q. What is the Civilian Conservation Corps and what part did they play in Rocky Mountain National Park?
A. Created by President Franklin D. Roosevelt on March 31, 1933—during the events of his First Hundred Days—the Civilian Conser-

---

Fall River Road is exceedingly scenic, but if you have an aversion to one-lane, one-way gravel roads that snake along precipices via exaggerated switchbacks, consider forgoing this old road and sticking to the more-modern Trail Ridge Road.

vation Corps (CCC) was created to battle job losses of the Great Depression. The official act that created the CCC was titled "An Act for the Relief of Unemployment Through the Performance of Useful Public Work." The first-ever CCC project took place in Virginia. Later the CCC began work on Rocky Mountain National Park, including road construction and general beautification projects.

Q. When did the Civilian Conservation Corps begin work on Rocky Mountain National Park?
a) December 10, 1931   b) May 17, 1933   c) March 9, 1938
A. b) May 17, 1933.

Q. How many men were originally attached to the Civilian Conservation Corps' Rocky Mountain National Park workforce?
a) 121   b) 137   c) 160
A. c) 160.

The CCC's Camp NP1-C.

Q. The Civilian Conservation Corps camp in Rocky Mountain National Park was designated camp NP1-C. What was so significant about this post?
a) It was the nation's first camp.
b) It was the only camp to have women workers.
c) It was the first camp located west of the Mississippi River.
A. Camp NP1-C was the first Civilian Conservation Corps camp located west of the Mississippi River.

Q. What other iconic Colorado landmark, near Denver, was a project of the Civilian Conservation Corps?
a) Red Rocks Amphitheatre   b) Garden of the Gods
c) Cherry Creek Reservoir
A. a) Red Rocks Amphitheatre in Morrison, Colorado. Red Rocks is an outdoor amphitheater where world-renowned musicians play

---

In the park, the Utility Area Historic District holds rustic buildings designed by the National Park Service and built by the Civilian Conservation Corps, many still used for their original purpose.

to jubilant crowds. Everyone from Elvis to The Beatles and U2 have played this much-storied venue.

Q. In what year was Trail Ridge Road, the byway that bisects the park, completed?
a) 1922   b) 1932   c) 1943
A. b) In 1932.

Q. What is the altitude of the highest point along Trail Ridge Road?
a) 10,083 feet   b) 12,183 feet   c) 13,945 feet
A. b) 12,183 feet, making it the highest paved *through-road* in the United States. The highest paved road in America leads to the top of nearby Mount Evans, near Idaho Springs, Colorado, but dead ends at 14,130 feet above sea level.

Q. How long is Trail Ridge Road Scenic and Historic Byway?
a) 48 miles   b) 52 miles   c) 57 miles
A. a) 48 miles.

Q. About how long will it take you to drive the length of Trail Ridge Road Scenic and Historic Byway?
a) An hour and a half   b) Two hours   c) Three hours
A. b) Two hours, though it's best to allot at least double that time if you plan on stopping and enjoying the scenery.

Q. In what year did the U.S. Secretary of Transportation and the National Byways Program designate Trail Ride Road an "All-American Road"?
a) 1987   b) 1996   c) 2003
A. b) 1996. The National Scenic Byways Program defines an All-American Road as "the roads to the heart and soul of America." In all, there are 31 All-American Roads located throughout the nation.

Q. Trail Ridge Road is one of how many nationally designated byways in Colorado?
a) 4   b) 6   c) 10
A. c) 10. The other nine All-American Byways in the state are Colorado River Headwaters, Dinosaur Diamond Prehistoric Highway, Frontier Pathways Scenic and Historic Byway, Grand Mesa

---

Ten backcountry buildings in Rocky Mountain National Park, made of stone or log, are on the National Register of Historic Places.

Scenic and Historic Byway, Lariat Loop Scenic and Historic Byway, San Juan Skyway, Santa Fe Trail, Top of the Rockies, and Trail of the Ancients.

Q. Trail Ridge Road is one of how many state-designated byways in Colorado?
a) 13   b) 21   c) 25
A. c) 25.

Q. How many miles of Trail Ridge Road rise above tree line?
a) 9 miles   b) 11 miles   c) 14 miles
A. b) 11 miles out of 48 are above tree line.

_____

Colorado's San Juan Skyway, in the San Juan Mountains,
is the state's other All-American Road, along with
Trail Ridge Road/Beaver Meadow Road.

DEATH, DISEASE & DISASTER

Q. In 1922, climber J.E. Kitts was killed by what on the summit of Longs Peak?
a) A lightning strike   b) A serious fall   c) Altitude sickness
A. a) A lightning strike. Though uncommon, a handful of lighting-related deaths have occurred in Rocky Mountain National Park, most at higher, exposed elevations. According to the National Weather Service, on average 62 people in the U.S. die every year from lighting strikes.

Q. In January of 1925, Agnes Vaille froze to death at the base of the North Face of Longs Peak. What happened to Herbert Sortland, the climber who attempted to save her?
a) He retrieved her body.   b) He also froze to death.
c) He never found her body.
A. b) After falling and breaking his hip, would-be hero also froze to death.

Q. Derek Hersey's climbing partner Carl Siegel died from a 500-foot fall while descending Longs Peak. What became of Hersey following the accident?
a) He never climbed again.   b) He summited Mount Everest.
c) He died in a climbing accident three months after the incident.
A. c) Unfortunately, Derek Hersey died of a climbing accident himself in Yosemite a mere three months after his climbing partner fell to his death on Longs Peak.

Q. In early summer of 1994, John Baise was guiding a climbing group up Hallett Peak when he slipped, fell and careened into his fellow climbers, causing one of the group—Amy Sweat—to fall 60 feet where she suffered back injuries. A helicopter was dispatched to rescue Sweat. What happened during the rescue?
a) The helicopter crashed into Hallett Peak.
b) The rescue team ended up saving another climber nearby.
c) Nothing, the rescue went off without any complications.
A. a) While attempting to rescue climber Amy Sweat after a fall, the helicopter sent to evacuate her crashed into Hallett Peak. Luckily, no one on board was injured. Unfortunately, the second helicopter sent to rescue Sweat was involved in another rescue a week later, also crashing while attempting the rescue, but this time killing all aboard.

Q. In 2003, Kurt Zollers fell do his death on the south side of Mount Baker. What was Zollers doing at the time?
a) Camping with his family b) Attempting to hang glide off the summit   c) Counting the bighorn sheep population
A. c) Kurt Zollers was working on a research project for Colorado State University to find out the bighorn sheep population in the area when he fell to his death.

Q. In 1980, John Link fell to his death near Thunder Lake while running. Why was he in such a hurry?
a) He was training for the Pikes Peak Marathon.
b) He was being chased by a mountain lion.
c) He was lost and began to panic.
A. a) He was training for the upcoming Pikes Peak Marathon.

Lightning is hot. How hot? In the right conditions, the heat generated from lightning can reach 50,000 degrees F—that's five times hotter than the surface of the Sun.

Q. In July of 1953, Kathryn Rees fell 150 feet to her death. Another member of her group, Sandra Miller, went for help. What happened to Miller?
a) She disappeared and was never heard from.
b) She fell to her death en route for help.
c) She came upon another distressed hiker.
A. b) In her hurry to find help, Sandra Miller slipped and fell to her death.

Q. What was climber Toby Cotter doing when he fell and suffered a fractured skull, arm and collarbone on Old Man Mountain?
a) Explaining to other climbers the importance of being roped in at all times

b) Camping on the edge of an exposed cliff
c) Making a first ascent up the north face of Old Man Mountain
A. a) Trying to bestow wisdom onto his fellow climbers, Cotter was demonstrating the need for a belay when his belay partner lost control of the rope and Cotter fell, sustaining injuries.

Q. While climbing Petit Grepon, Todd Marshall fell while still roped in and slammed into the side of the mountain, killing himself. What happened to his body?
a) It was quickly recovered by his climbing partner.
b) It slid down the rope to the base of the mountain.
c) It hung suspended along the cliff face for a number of days before being removed.
A. c) Because Marshall had died in a precarious location, his body hung just out of reach of rescuers for a few days before it could be reclaimed.

Q. In 2001, a climber was partially paralyzed while on The Spearhead. With the help of his climbing partner he was able to get down the peak. What was the cause of his partial paralysis?
a) A fall   b) A stroke   c) An animal attack
A. b) A stroke.

Q. In July of 2010, a Wisconsin man and his daughter crashed

In 2004, Richard Mercado lost control and was injured while sliding down Andrews Glacier on a plastic trash bag.

their plane into a remote section of Rocky Mountain National Park. What happened to the pair?
a) They both died on impact.
b) They walked away with only minor injuries.
c) One of the pair suffered life-ending injuries
A. b) While the small plane crashed in a remote and woody area of the park, both father and daughter suffered only minor injuries and were rescued by helicopter. The cause of the crash was said to be mechanical failure.

Q. How many airplane crashes have occurred in the park since it opened?
a) 6   b) 11   c) 17
A. b) There have been 11 airplane crashes in Rocky Mountain National Park resulting in 11 deaths.

Q. In 1943, what heralded World War II American bomber crashed in a remote part of the Mummy Range in Rocky Mountain National Park, killing all eight aboard?
a) B-17 Flying Fortress   b) B-24 Liberator   c) B-29 Superfortress
A. a) In October of 1943, a B-17 Flying Fortress, flying from Rapid City, S.D., to Denver, crashed into an 11,000-foot mountain, resulting in the deaths of eight crew members and starting a small forest fire.

Q. How many total mountain climbing deaths were recorded in Colorado in 2010?
a) 0   b) 10   c) 15
A. c) 15 climbing-related deaths occurred throughout Colorado, making it one of the deadliest years on record for Colorado climbers.

Q. What does the term "loved to death" mean?
a) An animal becomes so popular with hunters that it disappears from the local habitat.

A fatal airplane crash in Rocky Mountain National Park claimed two lives in 2000, near Comanche Peak, but for more than a decade afterward no more fatal plane crashes occurred.

b) A wild animal dies in a harsh winter because it has come to rely on human food.

c) An area is so popular with visitors, it eventually becomes damaged beyond repair.

A. c) An area becomes so popular with visitors it sustains excessive damage due to overuse. Rocky Mountain National Park constantly battles overuse in popular areas of the park. As a visitor, it's important to follow all national park rules and stay on designated trails to keep areas from being "loved to death."

Q. What natural disaster in 1976 resulted in the deaths of 145 park visitors?

a) Flood   b) Fire   c) Earthquake

A. a) Flood. On July 31, 1976, a torrential rainstorm descended upon Rocky Mountain National Park's Big Thompson Canyon, marring a previously cloudless day. The heavy downpour quickly raised river levels to heights cresting above nine feet. The added water volume was funneled through the canyon, gathering speed and flotsam and jetsam as it roared to lower elevations—where rain had not yet even fallen, catching lower-level park visitors by surprise. Boulders the size of cars, trees the size of school buses, and vast amounts of sediment were all carried along the river's gauntlet.

Everything caught in the path, including homes and businesses, was swept downstream with little effort. Because flood warning systems were virtually nonexistent in the 1970s, there was little warning for the locals as they sought cover and higher ground. The lack of warning, coupled with people's inherent curiosity that led gawkers to go dangerously close to the flood waters, resulted in one of the park's most deadly days.

Q. What 1982 natural disaster in the park resulted in the deaths of three people?

a) Flood   b) Fire   c) Earthquake

A. a) Flood. On July 15, 1982, an earthen dam crumbled, releasing more than 300 million gallons of water in a matter of moments. Built in 1903, the nearly 80-year-old dam lost a 95-foot-long section, causing the waters of Lawn Lake to surge in towering 30-foot-high walls of water through the park and onward to the town of Estes Park.

In 1982, Lawn Lake's flooding waters ran at the rate of 18,000 cubic feet per second at their fastest.

Q. Where today can visitors see the effects of the Lawn Lake flood of 1982?
a) Moraine Park   b) Horseshoe Park   c) Beaver Meadows
A. b) At Horseshoe Park, visitors can see the after-effects of the Lawn Lake flood. Here, boulders, trees and sediment have been displaced from farther up the park by flood waters. On this otherwise open plain, the waters began to disperse, depositing debris across 42 acres.

Q. How heavy is the largest boulder relocated to Horseshoe Park by the Lawn Lake flood?
a) 133 tons   b) 348 tons   c) 452 tons
A. c) The largest boulder weighed upwards of 452 tons (904,000 pounds); that's the same as 82 full-grown African elephants.

Q. What is an "alluvial fan"?
a) A prehistoric plant variety found in the park
b) A layer of sediment in the bedrock indicating the age of the park
c) The resting place of large amounts of debris carried by rivers or flood waters
A. c) An alluvial fan is created when river flows or flood waters subside and the debris carried by the currents settles in a fan-like pattern. When the Lawn Lake flood of 1982 retreated, Horseshoe Park became the site of a large alluvial fan.

Q. Which flood in the park caused a ripple effect, collapsing two dams and causing Fall River to flow through downtown Estes Park?
a) Big Thompson flood   b) Beaver Pond flood   c) Lawn Lake flood
A. c) Lawn Lake flood.

Q. What ill-advised act did two of the three people who died in Lawn Lake flood undertake?
a) They tried to kayak the raging river.
b) They tried to take pictures of rising flood waters.
c) They stayed in their homes, which were in the water's path.
A. b) They approached the flood waters with the intent of snapping pictures. Instead, they were swept away and quickly killed.

A person's odds of dying in a flood, earthquake, or other natural disaster are 1 in 3,357, odds of dying from a fall are 1 in 246.

The third individual who died in the flood was just unlucky, having set up camp near the Cascade Dam, the second dam to fail during the flood.

Estes Park during the Lawn Lake Flood

Q. What motivated park officials to acquire all titles to man-made reservoirs within Rocky Mountain National Park?
a) The spread of water-borne diseases
b) The threat of flood
c) Increased algae blooms
A. b) The 1976 and 1982 floods were the impetuses for the park to acquire rights to all reservoirs. Upon bringing every body of water back into the purview of the park, administrators began systematically dismantling any artificial dams, returning each high-mountain lake to its natural water storage capacity.

Q. What scientific benefit did the park's two large 20th century floods have for helping mitigate the effects of future floods throughout the world?
a) A better rain catchment system was designed.
b) Improved dam technology was created.
c) Better predictive flood models were made.
A. c) The Big Thompson Canyon and Lawn Lake floods led to predictive models for future floods. These models, created from water flow patterns and debris fields, help scientists and planners better determine the effects of possible flood-related disasters, with the hope of eliminating, or at least mitigating, their destructive force.

Both the 1967 and 1982 floods were declared federal disasters, enabling funds to be released for the park and nearby towns to use in reconstruction and improving safety features.

Q. What does high altitude have to do with your gas tank, and what is "vapor lock"?
a) High altitude turns gas into vapor.
b) High altitude causes your gas pedal to stick.
c) You get better gas mileage at higher altitudes.

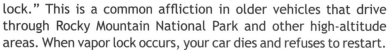

A. a) At high altitude, gasoline can turn to vapor—this phenomenon is called "vapor lock." This is a common affliction in older vehicles that drive through Rocky Mountain National Park and other high-altitude areas. When vapor lock occurs, your car dies and refuses to restart.

Q. How can you prevent vapor lock from happening?
a) Keep your gas tank close to empty.   b) Keep your gas tank full.
c) Use ethanol-based fuel.
A. b) Keep your gas tank full. If your car is prone to vapor lock, keeping a full tank helps reduce the chance of gas turning to vapor.

Q. How can you overcome vapor lock?
a) Start your car in reverse.   b) Stomp on the gas pedal.
c) Open your gas cap.
A. c) Open your gas cap. Vapor lock occurs when the gas in your tank turns to vapor, which is unable to travel down your fuel line into your engine. Opening the gas cap will allow the gas vapor to escape, leaving the non-gaseous fuel to make its way unimpeded to your engine. Luckily, most newer cars have specially designed gas caps to deal with vapor lock before it starts.

Q. While at a high elevation, people who experience breathing difficulties, nausea, headache and lethargy are most likely afflicted with what?
a) Mountain or altitude sickness   b) Rocky Mountain spotted fever
c) Lyme disease
A. a) Breathing difficulties, nausea, headache and lethargy are all symptoms of mountain sickness, also called altitude sickness.

Q. What's the most effective way to combat altitude sickness?
a) Stop and relax.   b) Take an aspirin.   c) Descend in elevation.

"Winter" fuel formulas used during summer months increase the chance of vapor lock.

A. c) To combat the debilitating effects of being at altitude, the best course of action is to descend in elevation as quickly as possible.

Q. How can someone lessen their chances of being afflicted by altitude sickness?
a) There is nothing you can do.   b) Take time to acclimate.
c) Take shallow breaths.
A. b) Before engaging in any strenuous activity at altitude, it's best to spend a few relaxing days at a comparable altitude in order to acclimate.

Q. Why isn't cotton the best defense against cold and hypothermia?
a) It doesn't retain heat when wet.
b) It is often ill-fitting.
c) It is too porous to defend against wind.
A. a) When wet, cotton does not retain warmth. Synthetics, wool products, and blends of the two are highly recommended for cold, wet environments like those found in Rocky Mountain National Park.

Q. How many cases of Colorado Tick Fever are reported annually in Colorado?
a) Fewer than 50   b) 50-100   c) 100-300
A. c) Anywhere from 100 to 300 cases of Colorado tick fever are reported in Rocky Mountain National Park every year, depending on that year's tick populations.

Did you know that Colorado Tick Fever is the most-contracted disease in Rocky Mountain National Park? Colorado Tick Fever is a viral infection transmitted by wood ticks. Unfortunately, there is no true cure for Colorado Tick Fever, and the best modern medicine can do is mitigate the symptoms, which include weakness, vomiting, headaches, rash, and sensitivity to light. If you're among the unlucky people who contract Colorado Tick Fever, don't worry too much—symptoms aren't deadly and run their course within a week.

Hypothermia can set in any time a person's core temperature drops below normal—no matter what the season!

Q. Since it opened, how many cases of tick-borne Lyme disease have been reported in Rocky Mountain National Park?
a) None   b) 57   c) 154
A. a) None.

Q. Why haven't there been any reports of Lyme disease in Rocky Mountain National Park?
a) The ticks' food source isn't present.
b) Lyme disease has been cured.
c) There is no Lyme disease in Colorado.
A. a) The ticks' food source isn't present. Mule deer are the only deer regularly found in Rocky Mountain National Park. Blacklegged ticks, which carry bacteria that causes Lyme disease, feed exclusively on white-tailed deer, and are therefore not found in the park.

Q. What is the name of the tick-carried bacteria that causes Lyme disease?
a) *Natranaerobiales*   b) *Borrelia burgdorferi*
c) *Magnetospirillum*
A. *Borrelia burgdorferi*, named for its discoverer, Dr. Willy Burgdorfer.

Q. What potentially fatal disease shares its name with the park?
a) Rocky Mountain flu   b) Rocky Mountain spotted fever
c) Rocky Mountain pox
A. b) Rocky Mountain spotted fever. But if you're worried about contracting Rocky Mountain Spotted Fever in the park you need not worry, you've actually got more of a chance outside of the park, as most cases are found along the eastern seaboard. Those infected from this tick-borne infection usually recover through a regimen of antibiotics. Only about 3% of those infected actually die from it.

Q. Which is not a symptom of the tick-borne Rocky Mountain spotted fever?
a) Spotted rash   b) Nausea   c) Extreme thirst
A. Extreme thirst. The hallmarks of Rocky Mountain spotted fever are headache, nausea, vomiting, aches in the stomach and

---

To protect yourself from ticks, wear long sleeves and long pants, and tuck pants legs into your socks. Light-colored clothing further helps you to spot any ticks hitching a ride.

surrounding muscles and a spotted rash that first appears on the hands and soles of the feet, then migrates to the rest of the body.

Q. Which is not a symptom of Colorado tick fever?
a) Loss of vision   b) Lethargy   c) Vomiting
A. a) Loss of vision. Head and body aches, lethargy, nausea, vomiting, abdominal pain and sensitivity to light are all symptoms of Colorado tick fever.

Q. How many search and rescue incidents occurred in the park in 2009?
a) 56   b) 168   c) 190
A. b) 168. In 2009, Rocky Mountain National Park tallied the fifth-most search and rescue missions within the park system, accounting for 7% of system-wide incidents. Grand Canyon National Park led the way with 309 incidents, accounting for 13% of all national park search and rescue missions. The second-most incidents occurred in New York's Gateway National Recreation Area (293). Yosemite National Park in California tallied the third-most search and rescue missions (231), and Lake Mead National Recreation Area in Nevada had the fourth-most search and rescues (197).

Q. According to park numbers, which sex is more likely to be the subject of a search and rescue in the park?
A. Males. Nearly 70% of search and rescue efforts are undertaken to help find lost men. Maybe they just refused to ask for directions.

Q. What is chronic wasting disease (CWD) and what impact has it had on Rocky Mountain National Park?
A. According to the Chronic Wasting Disease Alliance, CWD is a contagious neurological disease affecting deer, elk and moose. It causes the brains of infected animals to degenerate, resulting in malnutrition, abnormal behavior, loss of bodily functions

---

The only way to tell if an elk is infected with CWD is to perform a necropsy, or post-death exam. There is no "live animal" test for CWD in elk populations.

and ultimately death. Unfortunately, a number of elk and deer populations in the park are infected with chronic wasting disease.

Mad cow disease is related to chronic wasting disease (CWD). Several rare human diseases are also closely related to CWD, including Creutzfeldt-Jakob disease, which occurs naturally in about one out of every one million people worldwide. Fortunately for humans and domesticated livestock, chronic wasting disease has only been known to effect deer and elk.

Q. How do scientists test mule deer in the park for chronic wasting disease?
a) They take tissue samples from their tonsils.
b) They take multiple blood samples.   c) They take fur samples.
A. a) They take a tissue sample from the deer's tonsils. The Colorado Division of Wildlife performs the tests and tracks results statewide. Most samples are provided by hunters submitting samples to the DOW. During the 2010-2011 big game hunting season, 2,876 deer were tested statewide, while percentages of positive tests range from region to region, the population in and around Rocky Mountain National Park showed a 5 percent infection rate—the highest among Colorado's regions. In general, the southeast and southwest portions of the state were devoid of any CWD-infected deer.

Q. How do you cure an animal infected by chronic wasting disease?
a) Through inoculation   b) You don't, there is no cure.
c) With dietary supplements
A. b) There is no known cure. The only way to effectively deal with CWD and ensure it doesn't spread to other animals is to euthanize the infected animal.

Q. True or false: Left untreated, CWD would eventually disappear from deer populations.
A. False. Left untreated, chronic wasting disease would eventually kill off the entire deer population.

Q. What percentage of a deer population needs to be infected

The park's composting solar toilets, located in backcountry locations, require workers to shovel out the waste every summer. Work crews use llamas to help carry out the human waste.

by CWD in order for it to be in danger of dying out completely?
a) 5%   b) 10%   c) 25%
A. a) 5%.

Q. What percentage of deer in Rocky Mountain National Park are thought to be infected by CWD?
a) 5%   b) 25%   c) 50%
A. a) About 5%.

Q. What percentage of the park's deer mouse population carries the deadly hantavirus?
a) 0%   b) 19%   c) 27%

A. b) 19%. The potentially fatal hantavirus is transmitted to humans via rodents through contact with their urine, saliva or droppings. In fact, you can contract hantavirus by inhaling contaminated dust particles after disturbing an infected area.

Symptoms of hantavirus include fever, sore muscles, headache, nausea, vomiting and fatigue, and are often mistaken for flu. As the disease progresses, fluid begins to fill the lungs, causing shortness of breath. Left untreated, hantavirus can be deadly. In fact, about one in three people diagnosed with hantavirus dies.

Q. True or false: Some park rodents are most likely carriers of the plague.
A. True. The bacterium that causes the disease known as the plague is passed from animal to human via a flea bite from an infected carrier animal. There isn't an accurate count of plague-infected animals in the park, but the chance of contracting the disease is small. However rare contracting this disease is, according to the Center for Disease Control, people are more likely to contract the plague in the western states of New Mexico, Arizona, California, Oregon, Nevada, and Colorado.

The Ford Escape Hybrids donated to Rocky Mountain National Park by the Ford Motor Company emit just one pound of hydrocarbon for every 100,000 miles of driving. Compare that to the annual average for gasoline-only vehicles of 77.1 pounds.

Q. How many year-round employees does the park employ to take care of custodial duties?
a) Three   b) Five   c) Seven
A. a) Three: two full-time and one part-time employee. However, during the high season, custodial staff grows to around 15.

Q. How many cubic yards of trash are taken from park receptacles in a single year?
a) 1,200 cubic yards   b) 2,200 cubic yards   c) 2,800 cubic yards
A. c) 2,800 cubic yards—that's just slightly more than the volume of an Olympic size swimming pool. Rocky Mountain National Park is an active recycler, often partnering with neighboring towns to increase awareness and access to recycling programs, including a yearly collaboration with the town of Estes Park to promote the recycling of corrugated cardboard. With roughly one-third of all American household waste coming from packaging, targeting this favorite material of shipping companies makes a world of sense.

Q. How many toilets does the park's cleaning crew service every day during the height of tourist season?
a) 75   b) 150   c) 300
A. c) Nearly 300.

Q. How much toilet paper does the park go through every year?
a) 1,350 miles   b) 1,800 miles   c) 2,100 miles
A. b) 1,800 miles. That's enough single-ply to stretch from Rocky Mountain National Park to New York City.

Among other volunteer opportunities, the truly devoted can choose to work custodial rounds. Yes, that includes privy duty.

About the Author

John Daters is a Colorado expatriate who spent a number of years creating content for the Colorado Tourism Office, exploring high-mountain trails and kicking the cobwebs out of some out-of-the-way Colorado locations. John has authored two other books on the Centennial State and now resides a bit farther east with his wife, two dogs, cat, and soon-to-arrive son Evan—named for the Colorado mountain where his dad proposed to his mom.

Q. Where can you get answers to hundreds of questions about your favorite national parks?
A. In the National Parks Trivia Series!

WHERE CAN YOU FIND ANSWERS TO HUNDREDS OF QUESTIONS ABOUT DEATH VALLEY? HERE!

DEATH VALLEY TRIVIA

THE MOST INCREDIBLE, UNBELIEVABLE, WILD, WEIRD, FUN, FASCINATING, AND TRUE FACTS ABOUT DEATH VALLEY!

BY DON LAGO

WHERE CAN YOU FIND ANSWERS TO HUNDREDS OF QUESTIONS ABOUT THE GRAND CANYON? HERE!

GRAND CANYON TRIVIA

THE MOST INCREDIBLE, UNBELIEVABLE, WILD, WEIRD, FUN, FASCINATING, AND TRUE FACTS ABOUT THE GRAND CANYON!

BY DON LAGO

WHERE CAN YOU FIND ANSWERS TO HUNDREDS OF QUESTIONS ABOUT GRAND TETON NATIONAL PARK AND JACKSON HOLE? HERE!

GRAND TETON TRIVIA

THE MOST INCREDIBLE AND UNBELIEVABLE FACTS ABOUT GRAND TETON AND JACKSON HOLE!

BY CHARLIE CRAIGHEAD

WHERE IS A GREAT PLACE TO FIND 1,000 FACTS AND FIGURES ABOUT YELLOWSTONE NATIONAL PARK? HERE!

Yellowstone Trivia

THE MOST INCREDIBLE, UNBELIEVABLE, WILD, WEIRD, FUN, FASCINATING, AND TRUE FACTS ABOUT YELLOWSTONE NATIONAL PARK, CROSSWORD PUZZLES AND WORD GAMES TOO!

by
JANET SPENCER
The Trivia Queen

Illustrated by Vince Moravek

RIVERBEND PUBLISHING
WWW.RIVERBENDPUBLISHING.COM
PHONE 1-866-787-2363